Blessed by the
Presence of

GOD

Blessed by the Presence of

GOD

Liturgies for Occasional Services

F. Russell Mitman

THE
PILGRIM
PRESS
Cleveland

In memory of my parents, Glenna and Russell,
Organist and Elder,
who carried me into my baptism
and immersed me in the liturgical life of the church

Scripture quotations unless otherwise noted are from the New Revised Standard Version Bible, copyright © 1989 by the Division of Christian Education of the National Council of the Churches of Christ in the United States, and are used by permission.

The Pilgrim Press, 700 Prospect Avenue
Cleveland, Ohio 44115-1100, U.S.A.
thepilgrimpress.com

© 2007 by F. Russell Mitman

12 11 10 09 08 07   5 4 3 2 1

Library of Congress Cataloging-in-Publication Data
Mitman, F. Russell.
   Blessed by the presence of God : liturgies for occasional services /
F. Russell Mitman.
      p. cm.
   ISBN 978-0-8298-1753-9 (alk. paper)
   1. Occasional services. 2. Liturgies. 3. Worship programs.   I. Title.
BV199.O3M58 2007
264 – dc22   2006037282

Contents

Preface

In 1987 I published a collection of original worship resources that was titled *Worship Vessels: Resources for Renewal*. The intent of that volume was not only to provide worship leaders and congregations with liturgies for corporate worship, but also to provide some necessary educational pieces surrounding the worship acts and to offer some biblical, theological, and historical perspectives on those worship acts to help interpret how those acts might be used. That volume included collections of resources for the Lord's Day celebration of Word and Sacrament but also for what sometimes are called "occasional" services: baptisms, weddings, and funerals.

In 2005 the first part of that book with considerable additions and revisions appeared as *Immersed in the Splendor of God: Resources for Worship Renewal* (The Pilgrim Press). That volume is devoted solely to services of Word and Sacrament — namely, the celebrations that most congregations see as the main weekly services. It includes revisions of the introductory materials in the original 1987 volume.

This book includes, considerably revised and with many additions, the second part of the 1987 volume — namely, those services for special occasions in the cycles and seasons of congregations and their individual members. Since 1987 the culture in which we find ourselves has experienced significant changes in how it perceives its needs for the church's prayers and blessings. So has the church experienced monumental changes in its ministry and mission in and to this vastly different world. Yet the Gospel comes to us embedded in forms and language of ancient cultures and has been transmitted through almost two millennia of rich tradition. The church's hermeneutical task is to allow Scripture and tradition to speak to us on the horizon of today and to allow God to speak again the living Word for the living of these days. So, considerably revised and enlarged, this part two of the 1987 volume attempts in a different day and generation to be about its original intention: namely, the renewal of worship in our churches. My aim here, again, is not simply to provide a collection of worship resources but to provide the accompanying educational tools to help worship leaders and assemblies grasp how these were shaped by the tradition and how they may be integrated into congregations' liturgical life today. This does not intend to be a theology of worship. To those who wish to explore these matters in greater depth I suggest reading James F. White, *Sacraments as God's Self-Giving* (Nashville: Abingdon, 2001) as an accompaniment.

Nor do I intend this book to be a replacement for the rich and full liturgies that have been produced by denominations in the past twenty years. What is here is presented as supplements that, I believe, are in harmony with what one finds in the official books of worship. I have discovered in my consultations with congregations and in conversations with pastors and teachers that too often the denominational liturgies are simply ignored: "We aren't ready for such radical change." May what I offer here be for some an intermediary step in that long process leading from lethargy to liturgical renewal. And as any crafter of worship resources is fully aware, what's in the book will be adapted for local use. Liturgy must find itself in the local cultures of each assembly. No two churches — even in the same denomination — are alike, and for worship to be truly authentic, it must arise out of each unique community. It would be appreciated by me as the copyright holder if the adapter would give some recognition of the source of even the adaptation!

Also, since 1987 considerable improvements have been made in the desktop publishing tools and processes that congregations use to provide printed worship guides, generally called church bulletins. *Immersed in the Splendor of God* includes a CD-ROM of all the resources so that whatever is chosen for insertion into bulletin or other formats can be highlighted and copied directly into whatever is the customary format for a local congregation's corporate worship. This volume of services for special occasions also includes a CD-ROM of the resources for congregational worship that are part of the text of the book. The reason for the inclusion of this electronic medium is that for these services to involve congregational participation some kind of printed material or projection needs to be available for use by the worshipers. And since most hymnals do not include any or most of these liturgies, what is necessary for congregational participation needs to be provided in some kind of printed or projected format. Otherwise, this book, like many others, would become merely a minister's handbook and, therefore, hardly a tool for congregational worship renewal. Purchase of this book along with the accompanying CD-ROM gives permission for the copying of any of the resources on the CD-ROM without the need for further permission, provided the copyright permission printed on the copyright page of the book and on the CD-ROM is included in the bulletins or other worship formats. The keyboard accompaniments and choral settings also may be copied for use by accompanists and singers.

When liturgical resources are copied and inserted in worship bulletins, there is a tendency on the part of the preparer to move immediately to the CD-ROM and to copy and revise the liturgies for corporate use in his or her own worship setting. I hope that *before* inserting the CD-ROM into the computer, those responsible for crafting worship will read the accompanying introductions to each chapter in the book to gain the necessary background information and to explore the various options and ways the liturgies may be used.

I wish to thank the congregation of the First United Church of Christ in Carlisle, Pennsylvania, for providing me with sabbatical leaves for the writing of the first edition of this book and for allowing some of these resources to help shape the worship life of that congregation. I also owe my gratitude to the pastors and local church leaders of Pennsylvania Southeast Conference of the United Church of Christ for allowing me the opportunities to facilitate workshops in a variety of settings, to consult with them regarding worship renewal in the churches, and to craft liturgies for monthly worship in the Church House and seasonal gatherings of the conference. I especially thank the Conference Consistory of Pennsylvania Southeast Conference for granting me a sabbatical leave for the purpose of revising the content and enlarging the scope of the resources in this new edition. And, finally, my thanks go to Pastor Wanda Craner for reviewing the texts, to Pastor Joseph Irwin for his assistance in the preparation of the CD-ROM, and to John Eagleson of ediType for his editorial assistance.

Blessed by the
Presence of

GOD

Introduction

Blessings for Special Times

In the seasons and cycles of congregational life there are special times for rites and celebrations that mark these as holy events in the life of the congregation or in the lives of individual members. Traditionally these are called "occasional services," and they find their way into denominationally produced handbooks for ministers but rarely into the hands of the assemblies gathered to participate in those celebrations. I propose to use "special times" as the name for this genre of liturgies because to me the word "occasional" carries with it a certain sense of something that is unessential and maybe even trivial, such as one encounters while browsing through the section marked "special occasions" in a greeting-card store. Generally what one finds in the "occasional" bins are cards that don't seem to fit under other categories. Instead, I think that "liturgies for special times" better honors these as *special* seasons — not casual moments — in the lives of individuals and congregations in which something is intended to be effected both by human design and by divine involvement. They may be festive and celebrative times, or mournful and reflective times. They may be times when the assembly asks God to bless an individual and other times when that assembly observes a common experience of God's blessing. "Time" here is not the chronological measuring that gets clocked by mechanical and digital instruments, but "times" in the biblical and theological sense of *kairoi* — God's special times when God effects divine grace in ways that are beyond and outside the clockings of chronological time.

In the Bible and in the church's traditions — and to some degree in human expectations — these are perceived in faith as times of blessing. From God's promise to Abraham and Sarah, "I will bless you, and make your name great, so that you will be a blessing" (Genesis 12:2), to Peter's sermon on Solomon's Portico in which, quoting Genesis, he interprets God's blessing of Abraham as the sending of the resurrected Christ to change Abraham's descendants into a new community in Christ (Acts

3:25–26), God intervenes with divine grace to effect a special relationship that would not occur on its own. Each blessing carries with it a sense of setting apart, a making holy, by the action of a holy God. And each blessing also involves some human commitment to the covenant God initiates and some human participation in the blessing act. In Mark's version of the Passover supper Jesus "took a loaf of bread, and after blessing it he broke it, gave it to them, and said, 'Take, this is my body'" (Mark 14:22). Luke and Paul add Jesus saying, "...in remembrance of me." Luke adds that on Easter the risen Christ joined two disciples on the road to Emmaus, and, "when he was at the table with them, he took bread, blessed and broke it, and gave it to them. Then their eyes were opened, and they recognized him..." (Luke 24:30–31). The act of blessing the bread was not to transform the bread itself, but so that the blessed bread would become a consecrated sign to those eating it of the Christ eating it with them. In other words, the blessing is not just of the bread itself but of both the bread *and* those eating it. And in this eating (and drinking) of what is blessed, whenever the eating (and drinking) is done "in remembrance [*anamnesis*] of him," Christ is present with them. Luke concludes his Gospel with the ascending Christ's blessing: "While he was blessing them, he withdrew from them and was carried up into heaven. And they worshiped him, and returned to Jerusalem with great joy; and they were continually in the temple blessing God" (Luke 24:51–53). Christ blesses the community, and the community's worship is an act of blessing God, and both on the divine side and the human side the bless-word is the same, *eulogein,* literally, a "good speaking."

The church began to consider some of these times of blessing "sacraments," literally, "holy oaths or holy remembrances," generally instituted by Jesus, in which divine grace is imparted. By the time of the Protestant Reformation of the sixteenth century, the number of sacraments in the Roman Catholic Church was set by the Council of Trent (1545–63) at seven: baptism, penance, Eucharist, confirmation, matrimony, holy orders, extreme unction. The Protestant Reformers believed that only two were instituted by Jesus — baptism and Eucharist, or holy communion. Luther included the preaching of the word, and the Anabaptists remembered that Jesus also instituted footwashing, although they have not considered footwashing a sacrament. The other five — penance, confirmation, ordination (holy orders), marriage, and anointing (unction) — depending on the ecclesiastical tradition, either were relegated to the status of rites or simply forgotten. Some modern Roman Catholic theologians, while maintaining the traditional seven sacraments, now speak of a more general "sacramentality," believing that God can be encountered in more ways than just in the seven sacraments of the church. Protestants, on the other hand, while wanting to maintain the sacramental specialty of baptism and holy communion, also are inquiring whether the means of divine grace can be so restricted. Is not God's grace imparted through other rites and rituals, including prayer public and private? I will leave the debate about what constitutes a sacrament and how many sacraments there are up to those inquiring minds and the final decision up to God as to the ways in which God blesses God's people. The orders that are included here are simply my attempt to try to put into liturgical formats what Bible and tradition consider to be the ways in which people, in special seasons of their personal lives and in the life of the Christian community, seek to be blessed by the presence of God.

One of my friends, who is a Roman Catholic cardinal, during a visit of the pope to Cuba, found himself walking alone and noticed a group of a dozen or more boys converging on him. His initial reaction was one of apprehension, but he soon heard them calling to him as they ran toward him, "Father, bless me, Father, bless me, Father bless me!" Of course, he did bless them — with the sign of the cross. In what seemed to him to be a culture in which the church is so restricted and in which faith officially is viewed through Marxist eyes, nevertheless there seemed to be something in even the youngest of this secular population that needed to be in touch with a reality greater than what the culture could provide.

In my own observations and in my contacts, particularly with those under age thirty, I find emerging among them a search, in the words of Horatius Bonar's hymn, to "touch and handle things unseen." Each summer thousands of youth and young adults converge on the grounds of the Taizé community in France to sing Jacques Berthier's wonderful repetitive chants. Churches in mainline Protestant traditions here in the United States are beginning to hold special services accompanied by Taizé music, and it's interesting to find people of all ages, but particularly youth and young adults, so willing and eager to sing chants, some of which are in Latin!

In Berlin in the summer of 2003 during the first ecumenical *Kirchentag,* an assembly of hundreds of thousands, primarily composed of youth and young adults, each received a blessing of water and the sign of the cross on their foreheads while we sang over and over, "Ihr sollt ein Segen sein" ("You [plural] shall be a blessing"), and huge inflated red halos hovered over the places of blessing, including the Brandenburg Gate that once marked the horrible division between East and West. The theme of that

Kirchentag underlined to me that ritual is not an end in itself, as psychologically and spiritually engaging as it may be, but rather is a commissioning for discipleship and a sending into the world so that others may receive the blessing too.

All across North America, assemblies in which the average age is twenty-two find themselves in darkened sanctuaries immersed in listening to choirs dressed in cassocks and albs singing medieval chants. I participated recently in a Good Friday service of walking the stations of the cross in a very medieval-looking church, and I discovered that, among the two dozen or so persons on the walk, I probably was the oldest person present! The following evening my son, who was thirty-one at the time, accompanied my wife and me as we participated in the Great Vigil of Easter. It was a two-and-a-half hour service that moved from darkness and the lighting of a new fire and ended in festival Eucharist, complete with exceptional choral and congregational singing and readings from the Old Testament's salvation history, baptism and communion, candles and incense, bells and drums, and even shouts and loud applause when the pastor announced, "The Lord is risen!" My son's response was, "That is the best Easter service I've ever been to!" The preacher in his homily noted that the Great Vigil, one of the oldest liturgies in the Christian church, involves all five senses.

While some people are searching for worship experiences that engage holistically all the senses, many of our church leaders in mainline Protestantism are still functioning out of Enlightenment modalities that have reduced much of worship to exercises in speaking and hearing, practices that are meant to engage the hearer's reason so that a reasonable and responsible action will be elicited either on the part of the individual hearer (mostly) but also by the community of hearers. No wonder many people find what is so often labeled "traditional" worship boring! It is! — particularly to those who have become accustomed to the heightened-volume electronics and even pyrotechnics of the entertainment empire. There have been some leaders in the religious community who have believed that, in order to get drop-outs back into churches, liturgies have to adopt the techniques of the entertainment media. And in some cases their efforts have been successful — witness the growth of the so-called "megachurches."

Yet there seems to be a danger in such accommodations, and the question arises as to how lasting the "how-much-more-can-I-entertain-you?" approach will be. Some churches have invested six-figure sums in very sophisticated equipment that, in many cases, is used simply to project texts (that is, words to songs) or to enhance the amplification of the voices of the entertainers (preachers and choirs) to rock-concert decibels, or to provide high-wattage stage lighting to focus even more attention on the performers. All of this tends to create even more passivity on the part of the assemblies and more and more defines the worship leaders — including choirs — as entertainers. And underneath it is merely the same old leftover-from-the-Enlightenment appeal-to-reason speak/hear mode, but dressed up in expensive entertainment attire.

It is interesting to me that the religious fundamentalism that has captured much of the American religious mind and has bought into the entertainment gadgetry is based on a rationalistic epistemology — that is, a way of knowing — that, ironically, it simultaneously says it rejects. Fundamentalism's approach to the Bible essentially is based on a rationalism that has flattened language so that words essentially have one meaning. "The Bible says" approach assumes that words — even translated from one language to another — have only one meaning. All one needs to do is to read the words of the Bible as one would read the words of a telephone directory or a science textbook, and those words in themselves become truth. Poetic metaphors are reduced to rational propositions; multi-valent stories are reduced to scientific and historic facts. In the end, those who, for example, reject the scientific community's theories about how the world evolved simultaneously substitute a "creationism" founded, albeit in biblical texts, on the same kind of empiricism based on human reason that science uses to explain phenomena via the scientific method. By the way, American theologian John Williamson Nevin in 1843 (*The Anxious Bench*) made the same assessment of nineteenth-century revivalism — that its devices for conversion were simply another form of rationalism. Yet the imprint of revivalism is still imbedded in American cultural religion whether it be in the worship practices of religious fundamentalists or even of some Protestant mainline churches.

Worship, in such an atmosphere, although garnished with music and prayers of evangelical pietism and fervor, basically is shaped by the lecture mode — that is, essentially a sermon-lecture appended with some opening and closing exercises. Scripture is not read as a liturgical event prefaced by prayers that God will interpret them; instead the preacher asks the assembly to open their Bibles to read the proof-texts that he has chosen to give supposed theological credence to his argument. Music is not intended to help people become immersed in the splendor of God but to provide testimony to the performer's own religious experience. And the setting often is not a place meant to be set apart as God's holy place but that particular assembly's sound stage and auditorium (note the Latin root *audire*, "to hear") full of "multi-media" technology that only serves to intensify an

Enlightenment rationalism's speak/hear mode. Some religious communities even eschew the designation "church" either for the congregation or the building and call the place a "worship center" or other euphemism borrowed from a shopping-centered culture.

It is apparent to some of us in worship leadership that the lure of the entertainment mode is fading. What may have appealed to the baby-boomer generation rebellion now may be passé, and their children and grandchildren are searching for worship that is deemed far less artificial and person-centered and far more genuine and community-centered. There are some of us searching to get beyond the worship wars of "contemporary" versus "traditional" that have polarized churches and their leaders. What seems to be emerging is not a quest for more multi-media worship but worship that is more multi-sensory. It's not a matter of borrowing modalities from the world of entertainment but of discovering — sometimes recovering — ways for people to worship God that, in content and perception, are both traditional and contemporary, multi-sensory and multi-valent, and that allow individuals and congregations to find themselves touched and handled by things unseen, that is, blessed by holy mysteries that do not fit into the narrow canons of human rationality. It appears that more and more people are searching not to know more *about* God, but to *know* the God who moves in mysterious ways to perform wonders that fallible human beings can participate in and perceive as acts of divine blessing. Rituals have meaning in that they open us to realities that lie beyond the rituals themselves.

I once had a discussion with someone about the language of hymns. He insisted that words such as "above" and "up" in memory-bank hymns are leftovers from an age of a three-storied-universe and that in a day of a scientific understanding of reality, those words needed to be eliminated from the hymns. Likewise, he continued, words like "dark" and "walk" are cruel to people of color and people with physical disabilities, and therefore they would need to be changed. His thinking was like that of Nicodemus in his response to Jesus' statement in John's Gospel about being "born again." For the Greek word *anothen* can mean "again" as a second time chronologically, or it can also mean "from above" or "anew" as an action of divine initiation. "Above" here is not a spatial definition but a spiritual reality, and it is this second, or even third, meaning of which Jesus is trying to convince Nicodemus. The Gospel of John is full of words of Jesus that have multiple meanings: bread, vine, door, sheep, shepherd, life, and so much of the church's liturgical life has been built on these multi-valent metaphors. In fact, much of religious language in general is highly metaphoric, and to eliminate the metaphors is to flatten liturgy to an exercise in rational propositions. We need to keep the metaphors and teach people how to think metaphorically in order to help the Nicodemuses of a secular culture to become immersed in a God who is much bigger than our minds have been conditioned to think.

Moreover, multi-sensory experiences open up people to new ways of perceiving reality. The power of imagination with which we are endowed by our Creator soon gets programmed out of us by our educational and other social systems that are dominated by rationalism. Poetry that was memorized by previous generations and taught them how to think meta-phorically finds little space in current curricula. Music — and teaching students how to read the special language of musical notation — likewise is gone from most public schools. Art in which even the youngest of children can express themselves, even before they can speak, no longer finds enough priority for taxpayer dollars. As science and its technology have been elevated to premier status in education and society at large, it is natural that the current generation is metaphorically deprived. Yet music therapy and art therapy are now master's-degree specialties pre-scribed for those who are suffering from psychological disorders. It seems that eighteen-to-twenty-two-year-olds (80 percent of them in a recent sur-vey had never been inside a church) are searching for experiences that will nurture them out of their metaphoric and multi-sensory deprivation. We have four senses other than our faculties for hearing, and they need to be stimulated with metaphoric and multi-sensory therapies not only to help us experience human realities more wholesomely but also to help us be immersed in wondrous splendor of a God who comes to us in more ways than words.

All of the liturgies in this volume are shaped for those special times of blessing that have been part of the Christian experience, some from the earliest seasons of the church's life. Although they have been crafted from and for an essentially Protestant perspective, they try to recover in an ecumenical environment some of the multi-valent and multi-sensory expressions that were either forgotten by the Reformers or have been rebelled against as "too catholic" in a religious culture shaped by leftovers from the Enlightenment. Although Protestant noses generally have not been conditioned to appreciate the sweet smell of incense, perhaps by exposure in small doses (for example, frankincense on Christmas Eve) folks can begin to take in the splendor of God through their nostrils! Moreover, incense provides not only an olfactory experience; it also is a visual reminder of the presence of God (Isaiah 6:4). I can remember from my childhood the Holy Saturday aroma of the port wine in the trays of tiny glasses for holy communion and the smell of freshly baked bread the elders had cut into cubes for Easter Eucharist — all covered with a linen cloth on the altar — or the fragrance of the lineup of lilies that the Ladies Aid Society had placed along the chancel rail ready to herald the Easter resurrection. I still can remember *smelling* that Easter was coming!

But there are other nonverbals that are part of the multi-sensory palate. In the rites of Christian initiation there are the visuals of water being poured, the sign of the cross being placed, the laying on of hands, a candle being lighted. And there are the auditory communicators, verbal and nonverbal: the splash of water, a baby's cry, the "Amens" of the people. Some of the liturgies included here include orders for the celebration of the Eucharist with its tasting of bread and wine. When one feels the wine being swallowed, it becomes a symbol of the Holy Spirit entering one's inner being. And there are the visuals of the Eucharist: the elements carried to the table during the offertory, the bread being broken, the cup being poured, the sign of the cross. I once participated in a mass in a Roman Catholic church in the Netherlands, and, although I do not understand a word of Dutch, I knew what was happening by means of the visuals of the mass. I presume the same must be true for persons with hearing impairments. And for those with visual impairments, the meaning comes through hearing. And for those with both visual and hearing impairments — Helen Keller is the classic example — communication is through touch. These liturgies preserve and/or recover the rich traditions of touching that have been part of the Christian liturgical experience: anointing, laying on of hands, the embrace and handshake of the peace, the feel of water dipped into or sprinkled on the head, the texture of bread broken, the handling of the cup, the touch of a ring being placed on a finger, a towel wiping washed hands and feet. How much richer these acts of blessing become when opportunities are given for people to experience realities that lie beyond the hearing of words alone.

My intention in what appears in this volume is to allow some ancient practices to find a freshness that comes through the shaping of a new setting for these blessing acts, like the placement of a beloved old gemstone full of rich memories into a new ring fit for a new wearer. Some of this shaping has emerged through practical pastoral needs, some through finding new modalities for observances, and some through trying to be sensitive to the needs of an emerging generation of Christians, many of whom have not yet made their way across the threshold of a church doorway.

All of the liturgies, even though some may be focused on the blessing of individuals, are corporate acts of the Christian community. Hence, all are intended to be acts for public worship, and all involve the community as active participants in the liturgies. Some will find a place within a regular service of Word and Sacrament. Others will find settings outside the Sunday morning experiences of congregations, perhaps even outside the spaces that congregations claim as ones dedicated for the worship of God. Nevertheless, even in these settings, the sequenced ordering of the worship acts is the classic *ordo* of Christian worship, which has been part of the church's life from the very beginning and which is discernible in the patterns of worship in both Old and New Testaments. The structure of these liturgies for special times, even some of those that take place outside the Sunday morning service, follow that same *ordo:* gathering/penitence, word, offering/Eucharist, and sending. Hence, the liturgies for initiation and discipling, marriage, penitential washing, healing, and burial include optional orders for the Eucharist.

Although the word "liturgy" frequently is used for what is printed on paper, essentially liturgy is what happens when people worship God. What is printed on the paper or projected on a screen is simply there to assist people to do the liturgy, literally the "work," of worshiping God. The CD-ROM includes what is necessary for printing and projection. What else is necessary is a community yearning to be immersed in the mystery of God and to find themselves as ones blessed by this awesome God.

Chapter One

Initiation and Discipling

Including:

A Liturgy for Baptism, Confirmation, and Reaffirmation

A Liturgy for Remembrance and Affirmation of Baptism

A Liturgy for Eucharist at Baptism or Affirmation of Baptism

During the last forty years we have witnessed a renaissance of interest in the meaning of baptism. Prompted by earlier biblical scholarship and given impetus by the theological and liturgical renewal that took place as a result of the Second Vatican Council in the Roman Catholic Church in the late 1960s, the church began rediscovering the very central place of baptism in individual lives and in the life of the church. We came to the realization that for too long baptism had been relegated to the periphery of our worship and reduced in the popular mind to a pretty ceremony of baby dedication.

We learned, too, that history and practice have separated into a number of distinct rites what is theologically a unified act of initiation and discipling centered in baptism. Most denominational books of worship perpetuated this disjuncture with a number of separate liturgies: one for infant baptism, one for adult baptism, one for confirmation, and a number of liturgies for the reception of members depending on their status or non-status as church members. Yet, thankfully, we see recent evidence that the church is taking a second look at the organic unity of these acts, thereby raising the fundamental liturgical question as to whether they ought not to be celebrated with a common liturgy. The liturgy that I offer in this chapter is a single order that, depending on the circumstances, can be used for any or all of the various acts of Christian initiation and discipling.

This is not the place for a treatise on the meaning of baptism: there are shelves of volumes that explore this subject far better than I could do in this little chapter. It is sufficient to say that baptism is the act of the self-giving God in which we are signed and initiated into the covenant of God's forgiveness and grace, incorporated into the body of Christ, and commissioned in the church to corporate and individual lives of holiness and righteousness. All other acts — confirmation, reception, and rein- statement — are intrinsically remembrances and reaffirmations of the one baptismal covenant. They are human affirmations of the sacramental ac- tion of God we celebrate in baptism. Confirmation is the commissioning act that in the early church was conjoined with the act of baptism itself but that, because of historical accidents, got separated into a distinct act that in traditions celebrating infant baptism was postponed until later in one's life. On the human side, confirmation is the affirmation of a relationship signed and sealed through the gift of the Holy Spirit in baptism. The reception and/or reinstatement of membership is the renewal of a com- mitment to a belonging to Christ and the church effected once and for all time in baptism, regardless of the human attentiveness to or disregard of the vows. And the warrant to receive the bread and wine in the Eucharist is not having undergone the rite of confirmation nor the successful com- pletion of a six-week membership class but rather the one acceptance into the body of Christ actualized by God in baptism. Although, because of the perpetuation of traditions, it may be the peculiar practice of denomi- nations and congregations to punctuate some of the acts with intervals of time, nevertheless they all are organically one and should be celebrated as one act. A common liturgy celebrates the essential unity of confirmation and baptism that the early church intended. It also reminds all who make affirmations of Christian discipleship and commitment to the church that their belonging really has to do with a sacramental action first established by God in baptism. Furthermore, if baptism is the common ground that unites all Christians, an order that celebrates both infant and adult bap- tism, confirmation, and reception of new members may become a means of reaching ecumenical understanding.

There is also something very practical about a common liturgy. There are occasions in the life of every congregation, particularly in an era of in- creased secularization when individuals and families come from different ecclesiastical traditions or even with no church background, when in one particular group individual persons are initiated by more than one of the different acts. In small congregations, there may not be sufficient num- bers to have separate celebrations for the various categories of initiating acts. And then there is the matter of the assembly — not to mention the clergy — not having enough hands and fingers to flip around to all the pages of the worship book or hymnal. Thus the common liturgy allows for an integrated celebration that has much in common with the practice of the early church before size compartmentalized the congregational family.

Among the many presuppositions that underlie the liturgy for initiation and discipling in this chapter, two need to be examined here. The first is that the act has meaning only in the context of the corporate people of God — among the baptized — who themselves receive the candidates into their midst in the body of Christ. The idea of Johnny being "christened" in the family's rose garden or before the fireplace mantel over which hangs grandpa's picture makes a sham of baptism. For although there is a personal dimension to being baptized, at the same time the corporate aspect must not be forgotten or ignored. Just as we are marked as unique persons and identified with a name all our own, so also are we signed and sealed into the covenant people of God and engrafted into the corporate body of Christ. Also, as this liturgy tries to point out, the baptism of *one* of God's people is an occasion for all to be reminded of their baptism and to be renewed in their own individual lives as Christians *and* as the body of Christ in that particular setting. Church revitalization begins in baptism, and the church is constantly renewed in baptism's life-giving waters. Those assembled are not spectators to what's going on but participants in the act, praying, responding, and welcoming the candidates into the family of God's people. For this reason, the appropriate words and actions for congregational liturgical participation need to be printed in a bulletin format. The accompanying CD-ROM includes the liturgical expressions that can be highlighted, copied, inserted into a print format, and adapted for congregational use in a service of baptism or baptismal remembrance and affirmation.

The second presupposition is that the normative occasion for the celebration of the initiating acts is *within* the service of Word and Sacrament. There may be historical validity for the celebration of baptism as part of an Easter vigil, but that service, too, presupposes the celebration of the Eucharist and is organically tied to it. Other than for special services or extenuating circumstances, the rightful setting for initiating acts is a service in which the congregation is gathered to hear the Word of God and celebrate the Eucharist. This presupposition points out the sacramental relationship between the act of being received and the act of being fed, between being received once and for all into the body of Christ and being nourished continually with the body and blood of Christ.

When in a service of Word and Sacrament the baptismal acts take place is determined by one of two traditions. The more ancient tradition places the font for baptism at the entrance of the sanctuary, symbolizing one's initiation and entrance into the Christian community. Hence, the baptismal acts take place at the beginning of the liturgical action, during the gathering or initiatory rites and *before* the service of the Word. The practice of beginning worship in some liturgical traditions with the baptismal formula, "In the name of the Father and of the Son and of the Holy Spirit," serves as a reminder that all worship always begins and ends in baptism. If the order that follows is used at this place in the liturgical action, it should be preceded by a penitential act that includes confession and words of forgiveness.

In another tradition baptismal acts take place between Word and Sacrament, that is, *after* Scripture and sermon, before Eucharist. Hence, in this tradition the font is placed in the middle of or in front of the assembly, and the baptismal acts are a liturgical continuation of the *ordo* leading from the Word in Scripture and sermon to offertory and Eucharist.

The entire baptismal act, no matter which part or parts of it are celebrated, rightfully takes place at the font whenever possible. The font is a tangible symbol of our belonging in the church from beginning to end. It is suggested in the liturgy for Christian burial, beginning on page 155, that the casket or urn be placed beside the font and the officiant conduct the beginning and end of the service at the font. Too often, I have discovered in my travels to churches, the font is situated in some dark corner or alcove or is pushed out of the way when not in use or even is kept in a storage room. Some churches don't even have a font or baptismal pool, and instead they use a little shell or silver candy dish on the occasions when someone is baptized. The font (or pool) is a powerful symbol at the center of the Christian faith and ought to be physically central to the assembly. It is appropriate for water to be in the font, or to be poured into the font at the beginning of the worship event, so that those who desire may dip their fingers into it to remind them of their baptism. The symbol of God's life-giving waters should never be allowed to go dry.

In the liturgy that follows, the questions addressed to the candidates and the answers they call forth are statements of *intentionality*. Whether the questions are answered by the parents in the baptism of a child or by the candidates themselves, these statements signify publicly the *intent* of having the act administered. Parents and sponsors do not take vows for their children. Rather, they express their intent that the act be administered according to Jesus' commission, but in the realization that the efficacy of the sacrament ultimately lies in the wisdom and mystery of God. The intentionality questions and answers are on the *human* side of the sacrament. They presume that the appropriate catechetization has taken place in individual sessions with the pastor or mentors or in group study courses. The renunciations of the powers of evil that in some liturgies include a lengthy list of such evils here are summarized in but one statement that is both a renunciation of the powers of evil—which are beyond number in this world—*and* the one profession that, instead of a multitude of evil powers having control over us, Jesus Christ alone is Lord and Savior—Lord of us individually *and* Lord of the church.

The Apostles' Creed serves as the public affirmation of faith. This creed developed in the life of the church as a response to the threefold baptismal questions of faith in God, in Christ, and in the Holy Spirit. In the liturgy that follows, the creed appears in a dialogical form in which the assembly joins with the candidates to respond to the baptismal faith questions. However, until the creed is recognized as an expression of baptismal faith and not as a test for orthodoxy, churches that have historical aversions to creeds may substitute a congregational covenant. If it is the custom of the church to use the Apostles' Creed as a congregational response to the Word, the recitation of the creed may be delayed until the appropriate place in the baptism liturgy.

A welcome extended by the congregation to the candidates is an integral part of this act and should never be omitted. (Some think it odd to address a six-week-old baby, but isn't it the natural human response when we see a new baby to *talk* to him or her?) It may be appropriate for the minister or a member of the congregation to carry the child amid the congregation as a sign of this new member coming into their midst. I suggest that such an introduction occur *after* or during the congregational welcome and *before* the prayer and the administration of the water. The welcoming is a gesture that signifies that the candidates are welcomed not only into a particular congregation but also into the whole body of Christ of which that congregation is the local embodiment. It is also a pledge of the congregation's concern for the spiritual welfare of all newly initiated into the household of faith, adults as well as children.

The prayer following the welcome has its parallel in the Eucharistic prayer of the order for holy communion. It is a recollection of God's saving deeds in history—the creation, the calling of Abraham, the Exodus event, Jesus' baptism and death and resurrection, the pouring out of the Holy Spirit, and the founding of the church. This prayer, like the Great

Prayer of the Eucharist, is a prayer of sacramental remembering (*anamnesis*). It is also an invocation (*epiclesis*) of the Holy Spirit to effect baptismal grace in and through the sign of washing and to commission the candidate to a life of holiness. For example, just as God's establishment of the covenant with Abraham and Sarah called them to a corresponding responsibility of living in holiness and righteousness, so, too, those baptized with water and the Holy Spirit are called and commissioned, regardless of age, to a life of covenant responsibility in the church of Jesus Christ. The minister or a representative of the congregation pours the water into the font prior to the last petition, even if the water itself is not administered. The sound of the water splashing is a powerful nonverbal symbol. If baptism is not administered, the final petition is replaced by the appropriate alternative(s).

Even though the state's computer records our names at birth, it is still important that names be a part of the initiating act. In baptism, the naming is not so much a matter of legally giving a name as it is the symbolic act of giving us a personal identity. It is our "Christian" name, and with this very personal identification we are baptized in the "Name" of the triune God, who has identified with us in the covenant. The "Name" of this triune God is "Father, Son, and Holy Spirit" — three Persons in one Name. Until ecumenical consensus is reached on an alternative wording, anything other than the baptismal formula of Jesus' commissioning of the disciples in Matthew 28:19 ("Father, Son, and Holy Spirit") is, I believe, sectarian and may prohibit a baptism from being ecumenically recognized. The wording traditionally appears in two forms, one in the active voice, "(*Name*), I baptize you," and the other in the passive voice, "(*Name*), you are baptized." In the accompanying order the latter is chosen to signify that this is a sacrament in which it is the triune God who effects the baptismal grace.

Placing the sign of the cross on the candidate's forehead, with or without anointing with oil, is an ancient yet very meaningful act, marking one symbolically as Christ's own unique person. The Christian name is uttered again at confirmation as one who is confirmed in the baptismal covenant, and, if he or she later is reaffirmed or reinstated, again such reconnection with the Christian community is with a personal identity and a Christian name. There are some liturgies for the Eucharist in which, as the elements are administered to each person, the server addresses the person by his or her baptized Christian name: "(*Name*), this is the body of Christ given for you." Anointing with oil while placing the sign of the cross is a significant symbol at confirmation and renewal when, of course, water is not administered. We are washed with the water of baptism only once and for all time, yet the anointing with oil and the placing of the sign of the cross can be a repeated act that not only reminds us of our baptism but also continues to be a sign of God's blessing us and uniting us with our crucified and risen Savior. Hence, it is appropriate, along with laying on of hands at confirmation, to anoint confirmands and others who reaffirm their baptism with oil and the sign of the cross as a commissioning to faithful discipleship.

The laying on of hands (commissioning) in some traditions is delayed to the time of confirmation. But there is no reason why it also cannot be given both in baptism *and* in confirmation. The laying on of hands really is an act of blessing prayer — that the Holy Spirit will empower the candidate to fulfill the covenant responsibility. In my mind, this act of empowering can be repeated without abrogating the once-and-for-all aspect of baptism. The use of the same words at both baptism and confirmation may be symbolically significant. However, I have included alternate words for the commissioning to be used specifically for confirmation.

The most important physical action, of course, is the washing, and that means getting wet! Without prolonging the endless argument as to how one gets wet in baptism, I merely want to make it clear that the act of washing necessitates getting wetter than three drops of water from a rosebud dipped in a bowl can provide! To ensure that a baby doesn't come away from the font dripping, I suggest using a towel embroidered with a cross or other symbol of baptism to absorb excess water, and then giving the towel to the family or candidate as a reminder of baptism. If water is placed in the font a half hour before the service, it generally is stone-cold by the time of the baptism. No wonder the baby usually screams! The rubrics of the ancient *Didache* direct that if the officiant cannot provide cold and running water, warm water may be substituted. I like the substitution. Baptism is not intended to be a cold shower but an immersion into the warm bath of God's caressing grace. My recipes: for a baptism that occurs at the beginning of the service, fill a pitcher with *warm* water; for a baptism that will take place after Scripture and sermon fill a pitcher beforehand with *hot* water, and have a representative of the congregation carry it to the font at the time of baptism. If the water is not to be poured over the candidate's head and/or body, it may be poured into the font during the last petition in the baptismal prayer. In either event the temperature will be just right.

The initiation act concludes with a prayer of thanksgiving which, like that of the Eucharist, serves as a corporate way for the people of God to express thanks to God for the grace received through this sacramental action. The unison portion of the prayer becomes an act through which all the members of the congregation renew their commitment in the baptismal covenant. The order concludes with the exchange of peace and a doxology. The accompaniment for the doxology may be found on page 170. In some traditions, a candle is lighted and given to each candidate. This candle can be relighted on each anniversary of the candidate's baptism as a reminder of this special blessing event.

In the event that the congregation wishes to reaffirm their baptism at a time when there are no candidates for baptism, confirmation, or renewal, a separate order for the remembrance and affirmation of baptism may be found on page 27. There are occasions throughout the church year when the lectionary texts focus on baptism, particularly on the first Sunday after Epiphany, which is also known as the Feast of the Baptism of the Lord. These become appropriate times for the use of this particular order. It includes the ancient ritual of *asperges* (dipping evergreen boughs into water and sprinkling the congregation) or the variant of inviting persons to dip their fingers into the water in the font and make the sign of the cross on their own foreheads or on the foreheads of others. In either case these physical acts accompany the leader's words, "Remember your baptism and give thanks!"

A liturgy for the Eucharist that may be used in conjunction with initiating and discipling acts is included on page 30. It also may be used on those Sundays when worship is shaped by biblical texts that focus on baptism and when it is desirable to include the order for remembrance and affirmation of baptism referred to above. The keyboard accompaniment for the memorial acclamation ("Christ has died, Christ is risen, Christ will come again") may be found on page 170.

A LITURGY FOR BAPTISM, CONFIRMATION, AND REAFFIRMATION
CD-ROM 1.1.1

The minister(s) and candidates gather at the font. A suitable baptismal hymn may be sung.

Minister: *depending on which of the following is applicable*
In obedience to Christ's command to "go and make disciples of all nations and baptize them in the name of the Father, and of the Son, and of the Holy Spirit," today we shall:

administer the sacrament of baptism.

and/or celebrate the confirmation of the baptismal covenant.

and/or welcome those who come to affirm their baptism and unite with us in this congregation.

A representative or representatives of the congregation may introduce the candidate(s).

Minister: If anyone is in Christ, there is a new creation!

All: **Everything old has passed away;**
behold, everything has become new!   — 2 Corinthians 5:18, adapt.

Minister: For the promise is for you, for your children,
and for all who are far away,

All: **everyone whom the Lord our God calls.**   — Acts 2:30

Minister: In the sacrament of baptism God accepts us
into the eternal covenant of forgiving grace
and initiates us into the body of Christ.
Through this sacred sign and seal we are marked and identified
as ones who bear Christ's name
and are welcomed as brothers and sisters into Christ's church.
Through confirmation and affirmation of our baptism
we are commissioned by the Holy Spirit,
and we renew our commitment to life together as the body of Christ.

Minister: Let us join with the whole church in all times and places in confessing our faith in the triune God.

The congregation may stand.

Minister: Do you believe in God?

All: **I believe in God, the Father almighty,**
creator of heaven and earth.

Minister: Do you believe in Jesus Christ?

All: **I believe in Jesus Christ, God's only Son, our Lord,**
        who was conceived by the Holy Spirit,
        born of the Virgin Mary,
        suffered under Pontius Pilate,
        was crucified, died, and was buried;
        he descended to the dead.
        On the third day he rose again;
        he ascended into heaven,
        he is seated at the right hand of the Father,
        and he will come to judge the living and the dead.

Minister: Do you believe in the Holy Spirit?

All: **I believe in the Holy Spirit,**
        the holy catholic church,
        the communion of saints,
        the forgiveness of sins,
        the resurrection of the body,
        and the life everlasting. Amen.

The congregation may be seated.

The minister asks the appropriate question(s) of the candidate(s).

Baptism

Minister: (*Name[s]*) _____ ,
        in presenting yourself to receive baptism with water and the Holy Spirit,
        do you renounce the powers of evil,
        and do you profess that Jesus Christ is Lord?

Response of candidate(s): I do, with the help of God.

Minister: Will you continue in the apostles' teaching and community,
        in the breaking of bread, and in the prayers?

Response of candidate(s): I will, with the help of God.

Minister: Will you strive for justice and peace among all people
        and respect the dignity of every human being?

Response of candidate(s): I will, with the help of God.

And/Or
Baptism of a Child or Children

Minister: (*Name[s]*) _____ ,
in presenting your *child/children* to receive baptism
with water and the Holy Spirit,
do you renounce the powers of evil,
and do you profess that Jesus Christ is Lord?

Response of parents and sponsors: I do, with the help of God.

Minister: Do you promise, by your words and deeds,
to help your *child/children*
grow in the knowledge and love of Christ
and in faithfulness to his church?

Response of parents and sponsors: I do, with the help of God.

And/Or
Confirmation

Minister: (*Name[s]*) _____ ,
in presenting yourself to be confirmed in the covenant of baptism
and to be commissioned by the Holy Spirit
for discipleship in God's world,
do you renounce the powers of evil,
and do you profess that Jesus Christ is Lord?

Response of candidate(s): I do, with the help of God.

Minister: Will you continue in the apostles' teaching and community,
in the breaking of bread, and in the prayers?

Response of candidate(s): I will, with the help of God.

Minister: Will you strive for justice and peace among all people
and respect the dignity of every human being?

Response of candidate(s): I will, with the help of God.

And/Or
Reaffirmation and Renewal

Minister: (*Name[s]*) _____ ,
in renewing your commitment to the church of Jesus Christ,
do you affirm the covenant of grace
God once made with you in your baptism,
and do you promise to participate faithfully
in the life and mission of this congregation?

Response of candidate(s): I do, with the help of God.

During the following act of welcoming, the minister or representative(s) of the congregation may carry the child/children into the midst of the assembly:

Minister: People of God, let us offer our welcome.

All: **We receive you joyfully into our common life.**
We enfold you in our care.
We pledge to grow with you in the knowledge and love of God.
Grace and peace to you in fullest measure.

The congregation may be seated.

Minister: The Lord be with you.

All: **And also with you.**

Minister: Let us pray.

> We give thanks, Holy God, that before the world was shaped and formed,
> your spirit moved over the face of the waters,
> and from the chaos of the deep
> you called forth order and life.

> We remember how by your loving hand
> you led the sons and daughters of Abraham and Sarah
> through the deep waters from bondage to freedom
> and marked them a holy people
> with the sign of your everlasting covenant.

> We rejoice that in the fullness of time you gave us Jesus,
> the child of Mary and Joseph, your beloved Son, our Lord and Christ.
> We remember John baptizing him in the water of the Jordan,
> the Spirit descending upon him like a dove,
> and the offering of himself to free us from sin and death
> and to lead us to everlasting life.

> We thank you that by the washing with water
> and the outpouring of the Holy Spirit
> we are baptized into the covenant of your grace,
> made one with Christ and his church,
> and commissioned to show forth his love in word and deed.

The minister or representative of the congregation pours the water into the font. Then the minister continues with any or all of the following petitions.

Baptism:

> We ask you to sanctify *this person/these persons/this child/these children*
> whom we baptize according to the command of our Lord Jesus Christ,
> and to bless this water that it may be the sign and seal
> of new life in his name.

Confirmation:

> Through the powerful benediction of your Holy Spirit,
> descend upon the one(s) who receive(s) the laying on of hands,
> that *he/she/they* may be confirmed in the covenant of baptism
> and commissioned for service in the name of Christ.

Reaffirmation:

> Strengthen the faith of all your people
> and especially of the one(s) who renew(s)
> *his/her/their* baptismal commitment,
> that your love may increase among all people,
> and the church of Jesus Christ may be a faithful witness in all the world.

All   **Amen.**

If oil is used for anointing, the minister may pray the following:

Minister: Bless, O God, this oil, pressed from earth's precious plantings,
            that it may be a sign to *him/her/those* who will receive it
            of your abundant blessing and anointing grace in Jesus Christ.

All: **Amen.**

Baptism

Minister: What is *your/your* child's name?

Candidate/parent/sponsor:
            (*Christian name only, not the surname*) ————————— .

Minister: *As the water is administered, candidates who are adults or older children may*
            stand or kneel at the font.
            (*Christian name*) —————————,
            you are baptized in the name of the Father and of the Son
            and of the Holy Spirit.

Candidate(s) and congregation: Amen.

As the sign of the cross is placed on the forehead(s) of the candidate(s), with or without
anointing with oil:

Minister: By this sacred sign may you be marked as a unique person
            belonging in life and in death to Christ crucified and risen.

As hands are placed on the head(s) of the candidate(s):

Minister: (*Christian name*) —————————,
            as *I/we* lay hands on you, we pray God to grant you the Holy Spirit,
            filling you with all grace and power to be a faithful disciple of Jesus Christ.

Candidate(s) and congregation: Amen.

Confirmation

Minister: *As hands are placed on the candidate(s) head(s)*
         (*Christian name*) _____ ,
         as *I/we* lay hands on you, we pray that the Holy Spirit
         may confirm you in the covenant of baptism,

Oil may be placed on the forehead(s) of the candidate(s) with the sign of the cross

         anoint you with this holy sign,
         and commission you to be a faithful disciple of Jesus Christ.

Candidate(s) and congregation: Amen.

Confirmation and Renewal

Minister(s) and congregational leader(s): *extending a hand of welcome or embracing*
         (*Christian name*) _____ ,
         I/we extend to you the right hand of Christian love of this congregation.

In all acts the service continues:

Minister: The peace of Christ be with you.

All: **And also with you.**

The assembly may exchange expressions of peace. The act may conclude with the lighting and presentation of a candle, the presentation of a towel and a certificate to each candidate, a welcome extended by representatives of the congregation, and the following:

Minister: Praise the Lord!

All: **The Lord be praised!**

Minister: With a joy beyond our human understanding we thank you, O God,
         for calling us your children and for making us heirs of your covenant.
         We rejoice that through baptism with water and the Holy Spirit
         we are named your sons and daughters
         and are received into the body of Christ.
         Nourish the precious gift of faith in your people,
         that what is sown in us by your grace may flower and bear fruit abundantly.
         And when death comes, grant us to share with all your saints
         in that life which has no end,
         through the resurrection of our Lord Jesus Christ.

All: **Remind us always of your promises given us in our baptism,**
         and renew our commitment to love you
         with heart and mind and soul and strength,
         and to love our neighbors as ourselves. Amen.

Minister: Now to the One who by the power at work within us
is able to accomplish abundantly far more
than all we can ask or imagine,

All: **to God be glory in the church**
and in Christ Jesus to all generations,
forever and ever. Amen. —Ephesians 3:20–21, adapt.

Words: Revelation 7:12, adapt.; Music: © 2005 F. Russell Mitman

The service continues with the prayers of the people, the offering, a prayer of thanksgiving, or the liturgy for the Eucharist.

A LITURGY FOR REMEMBRANCE AND AFFIRMATION OF BAPTISM
CD-ROM 1.2.1

This act may follow the sermon. A hymn may be sung, and the leader(s) gather at the font.

Leader: In Christ you have heard the word of truth, the gospel of your salvation, and were marked with the seal of the promised Holy Spirit.

All: **This is the pledge of our inheritance as God's own people.**
—Ephesians 1:13–14, adapt.

Leader: Let us confess the faith of our baptism.

The congregation may stand.

Minister: Do you believe in God?

All: **I believe in God, the Father almighty,**
creator of heaven and earth.

Minister: Do you believe in Jesus Christ?

All: **I believe in Jesus Christ, God's only Son, our Lord,**
who was conceived by the Holy Spirit,
born of the Virgin Mary,
suffered under Pontius Pilate,

was crucified, died, and was buried;
he descended to the dead.
On the third day he rose again;
he ascended into heaven,
he is seated at the right hand of the Father,
and he will come to judge the living and the dead.

Minister: Do you believe in the Holy Spirit?

All: **I believe in the Holy Spirit,**
the holy catholic church,
the communion of saints,
the forgiveness of sins,
the resurrection of the body,
and the life everlasting. Amen.

Minister: Do you reaffirm your renunciation of the powers of evil,
and do you renew your profession that Jesus Christ is Lord?

All: **I do with the help of God.**

Minister: Will you continue in the apostles' teaching and community,
in the breaking of bread, and in the prayers?

All: **I will with the help of God.**

Minister: Will you continue to strive for justice and peace among all people
and respect the dignity of every human being?

All: **I will with the help of God.**

Minister: Let us pray.

We give thanks, Holy God, that before the world was formed,
your spirit moved over the face of the waters
and from the chaos of the deep you created order and life.

We remember how by your guiding hand
you led the sons and daughters of Abraham and Sarah
through the deep waters from bondage to freedom
and marked them a holy people
with the sign of your everlasting covenant.

We rejoice that in the fullness of time you gave us Jesus,
the child of Mary and Joseph,
your beloved Son, our Lord and Christ.

We remember John baptizing him in the water of the Jordan,
the Spirit descending upon him like a dove,
and the offering of himself to free us from sin and death
and to lead us to everlasting life.

We thank you that by the washing with water
and the outpouring of the Holy Spirit
we are baptized into the covenant of your grace,
made one with Christ and his church,
and commissioned to show forth his love in word and deed.

The minister or leader may pour water into the font.

We ask you to bless us and this water
that it may be to us an affirming sign of our baptism into Christ
and a reminder of your promise of cleansing and forgiving grace.

All: **We thank you that you have claimed us as your own in baptism**
and have rebirthed us anew through the Holy Spirit.
Renew our commitment to love you
with heart and mind and soul and strength,
and to love our neighbors as ourselves. Amen.

The minister and/or other leaders may dip evergreen branches into the water and sprinkle
the water over the congregation. Or the congregation may be invited to come to the font,
dip their hands into the water, and make the sign of the cross on their own foreheads or on
the foreheads of others. As the asperges *(sprinkling) takes place, the minister and/or leaders*
may address each person or the assembly, saying:

Minister: Remember your baptism and give thanks!

All: **Amen.**

The service continues:

Minister: By baptism we have been buried with Christ into death,
so that, just as Christ was raised from the dead,
so we too might walk in newness of life.   — Romans 6:4

All: **Thanks be to God!**

Minister: Blessing and glory and wisdom and thanksgiving and honor
and power and might be to our God forever and ever!

All: **Amen.**   — Revelation 7:12, adapt.

Or singing

Words: Revelation 7:12, adapt.; Music: © 2005 F. Russell Mitman

The act may conclude with the exchange of peace and a hymn. The offertory and Eucharist
may follow.

A LITURGY FOR
EUCHARIST AT BAPTISM
CD-ROM 1.3.1

Minister: Lift up your hearts!

All: We lift them to the Lord!

The congregation may stand.

Minister: Lord Jesus Christ, to all who receive you,
            you give power to become children of God,
            initiating them through the Holy Spirit into your body,
            and commissioning them to lives of faith and service.

            We remember that on the night you were betrayed,
            you took bread and blessed and broke it
            and gave it to those at table with you, saying,
            "Take and eat, this is my body given for you;
            do this in remembrance of me."

            And after supper you took the cup and said,
            "Take and drink, this cup is the new covenant in my blood;
            do this as often as you drink it, in remembrance of me."

            On the day of resurrection, the first day of the week,
            when you were at table with two of the disciples,
            you took bread, blessed and broke it, and gave it to them.
            Then their eyes were opened, and they recognized you.

All: Lord Jesus Christ, in our baptism
            we have been buried with you into death,
            so that, just as you were raised from the dead,
            so we too might walk in newness of life.

Minister: Great is the mystery of faith:

All: *singing*

Christ has died, Christ is ris - en, Christ will come a - gain!

Music: F. Russell Mitman, 2005

Minister: Lord Jesus Christ, with the power of the Holy Spirit,
            bless us, and bless these gifts of bread and wine that we offer you,
            together with the offering of our very selves to you.
            Set these elements apart from a common to a sacred use,

that they may be the means of communion with you
in your body and blood
and in communion with all those
who have gone before us in the faith
and now surround us in our Christian course.
Set us apart as your holy people, ready here and now
to be your witnesses in a world crying for justice, mercy, and peace.

All: **Amen.**

Please be seated.

Intercessions may be prayed, if not previously included, and all may pray the Lord's Prayer.

Minister: *breaking the bread*
In the breaking of this bread we are one with Christ
in his body broken for us.

pouring the cup
In the pouring of this cup we are one with Christ
in his blood poured out for us.

Minister: Come, for all things are ready.

All: **Lord Jesus Christ, we come to this table to know you
in the breaking of this bread.**

The communion is served. After all have received, the service continues:

Thanksgiving

The congregation may stand.

Minister: Lord Jesus Christ, you have fed us at this table
with mysteries to nourish us in our baptismal belonging to you
and to those you have called out as our sisters and brothers in faith.

All: **Continue to breathe on us the Holy Spirit
that we may become more and more a reconciling community,
eager to forgive others and to receive the forgiveness
that we yearn so deeply to receive from them. Amen.**

The service may continue with a hymn of commissioning, followed by:

Minister: Go into all the world and proclaim the good news to every creature,
spread the saving word that God is near with wholeness and peace,
and announce to every one Christ's eternal promise:
"Lo, I am with you always, even to the end of time."

All: **Amen, Lord Jesus! Amen!**

Minister: Go with Christ's commission to make disciples of all nations,
teaching them to observe all that Christ has commanded.

The following may be accompanied by the sign of the cross:

Go under the sign of your baptism
and with the blessing of the Triune God — Father, Son, and Holy Spirit —
now and forevermore.

All: **Amen.**

Chapter Two

Morning Prayer

This liturgy for morning prayer is precisely that — a liturgy of prayer. Even the Psalms and hymn are themselves prayers and should be approached prayerfully. That, however, does not mean solemnly! The reading of Scripture, in this case prefaced with the prayer of illumination from Psalm 143, can become an act of prayer. Care should be given that a homily also is approached in the spirit of prayer.

The service is meant to be brief, and, except for the reading of Scripture, an optional homily, and a final hymn or Psalm, it is designed for use without much variation. Daily morning prayer is not part of most mainline Protestant church communities. However, I have discovered that there are a few congregations who have incorporated morning prayer weekly in Lent and, even fewer, every day during Holy Week. The liturgy here also may be used for opening worship in church meetings that begin in the morning. In some hymnals, the musical responses and Psalms for morning and evening prayer are located elsewhere than in the liturgies themselves, necessitating verbal rubrics ("Please turn to page _____ ."), and hence the flow of the liturgical action is interrupted. This liturgy is intended to be prayed and sung without directions and interruptions so that it may be the people's offering and so that the leader(s) will not interfere with the liturgical action. Truly, liturgy is the work of the whole assembly, and the role of the leader(s) is to facilitate the liturgical work. The initial gathering call may be spoken by three leaders seated throughout the assembly. The liturgy may be copied as a whole from the CD-ROM, and bulletins or worship folders may be created that can be used over and over. Everything for the assembly's participation is included.

From the beginning of the church's life, daily prayer involved the recitation of certain Psalms juxtaposed with Christians hymns and canticles and readings from the New Testament Scriptures. I have attempted to preserve that rich heritage in this liturgy for morning prayer as well as its complement in the service for evening prayer in the next chapter. Traditionally liturgies for morning prayer have included the Benedictus, the song of

Zechariah, as recorded in Luke 1:69–79. There are a variety of wonderful contemporary metrical settings that may be included here. Suggestions are: "Now Bless the God of Israel" by Ruth Duck, "Blest be the God of Israel" by James Quinn, "Bless'd be the God of Israel" by Carl P. Daw Jr., and "Blest be the God of Israel" by Michael A. Perry. All are set to familiar hymn tunes. A responsive-style prayer paraphrase of the Scriptural text of the Benedictus is provided here.

The musical portions of this service are so designed that, if keyboard accompaniment is not available, the Psalms, hymns, and canticles may be sung a cappella. A simple two-part accompaniment for keyboard or two instruments for the response to Psalm 139 may be found on page 171, and the keyboard accompaniment for the Kyrie (Lord have mercy) may also be found on page 171.

A LITURGY FOR MORNING PRAYER
CD-ROM 2.1.1

A nonverbal call to prayer may be issued by the blowing of a ram's horn or a conch shell. A bell also may be used to call the assembly to prayer.

Leader: Awake, my soul!

Brief silence

Leader: Awake, O harp and lyre!

Brief silence

Leader: Awake the dawn!

All: **I will give thanks to you, O Lord, among the peoples,
and I will sing praises to you among the nations.**

Leader: For your steadfast love is higher than the heavens,
and your faithfulness reaches to the clouds.

All: **Be exalted, O God, above the heavens,
and let your glory be over all the earth.**   —Psalm 108:1b–5, adapt.

A candle is lighted.

The assembly may sing, several times repeated, if desired:

PUER NOBIS NASCITUR

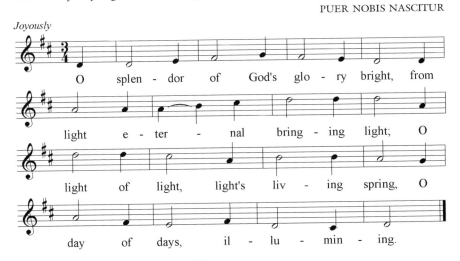

Joyously

O splen - dor of God's glo - ry bright, from light e - ter - nal bring - ing light; O light of light, light's liv - ing spring, O day of days, il - lu - min - ing.

Words: Ambrose of Milan (c. 340–c. 397);
Music: from "Piae Cantiones," 1582, adapt. Michael Praetorius, 1609

Or

Holy, holy, holy, God the Almighty!
Early in the morning we praise your majesty.
Holy, holy, holy, Merciful and mighty!
God in three persons, blessed Trinity!

NICAEA

Words: Reginald Heber, 1826; Word alterations © 1993 The Pilgrim Press.
Used by permission of The Pilgrim Press.

Leader: Almighty God, unto whom all hearts are open,
all desires known, and from whom no secrets are hid,
cleanse the thoughts of our hearts
by the inspiration of your Holy Spirit,
that we may perfectly love you,
and worthily magnify your holy name;
through Christ our Lord.

All: **Amen.** *—Book of Common Prayer,* adapt.

The assembly may pray the following Psalter prayer from Psalm 139 in unison with or without the musical response.

Response:

Lord, you have searched me and known me.

O Lord, you have searched me and known me.
You know when I sit down and when I rise up;
you discern my thoughts from far away.
You search out my path and my lying down,
and are acquainted with all my ways.
Even before a word is on my tongue,
O Lord, you know it completely.
Such knowledge is too wonderful for me;
it is so high that I cannot attain it. *Response*

Where can I go from your spirit?
Or where can I flee from your presence?
If I ascend to heaven, you are there!
If I make my bed in Sheol, you are there!
If I take the wings of the morning
and settle at the farthest limits of the sea,
even there your hand shall lead me,
and your right hand shall hold me fast. *Response*

Search me, O God, and know my heart;
test me and know my thoughts.
See if there is any wicked way in me,
and lead me in the way everlasting. *Response*

Words: Psalm 139:1–4, 6–10, 23–24; Music: F. Russell Mitman, 2004

A period of silence may be observed for individual penitence, followed by:

Leader: Let us pray.

All: O God, let me hear of your steadfast love in the morning,
            for in you I put my trust.
            Teach me the way I should go,
            for to you I lift up my soul.

                                                              — Psalm 143:8, adapt.

Leader: Listen for the Word of God in a reading from ——————— .

One or more passages of Scripture are read, each followed by:

Leader: The Word of the Lord.

All: **Thanks be to God.**

Silence or a brief homily may follow.

The assembly may sing a musical setting of the Benedictus (Canticle of Zechariah) or speak responsively the following prayer paraphrase:

Leader: Blessed be the Lord God of Israel,

All: **for you have looked favorably on your people and redeemed them.**

Leader: You have raised up a mighty savior for us
              in the house of your servant David,
              as you spoke through the mouth of your holy prophets from of old,

All: **that we would be saved from our enemies
              and from the hand of all who hate us.**

Leader: Thus you have shown the mercy promised to our ancestors,
              the oath that you swore to our ancestor Abraham,

All: **to grant us that we, being rescued from the hands of our enemies,
              might serve you without fear, in holiness and righteousness
              before you all our days.**

Leader: And your child will be called the prophet of the Most High;
              for he will go before you to prepare your ways,

All: **to give knowledge of salvation to your people
              by the forgiveness of our sins.**

Leader: By your tender mercy, O God,
              the dawn from on high will break upon us,

All: **to give light to those who sit in darkness and in the shadow of death,
              to guide our feet into the way of peace.**
              — Luke 1:69–79, paraphrased

Leader: The Lord be with you.

All: **And also with you.**

Leader: That whatever we think and say and do this day
          will be acceptable and well-pleasing in your sight,

All: *singing or speaking*

                    Lord,   have   mer - cy   on   us.

Leader: That we may forgive others this day
          as in Christ you have forgiven us,

All: *singing or speaking*
           Lord, have mercy on us.

Leader: That we may live in harmony with all creation this day
          and honor the unique integrity of every human being,

All: *singing or speaking*
           Lord, have mercy on us.

Leader: That all who need you in special ways this day,
          especially (*Name[s]*) _____,
          may find your comforting presence close to them,

All: *singing or speaking*
           Lord, have mercy on us.

Other intercessions may be offered, followed by silence.

Leader: Hear our prayers, O Lord;

All: **give ear to my supplications in your faithfulness;**
           answer me in your righteousness.   —Psalm 143:1–2, adapt.

(continued on next page)

All: *singing or speaking, with or without periods of silence between each petition*

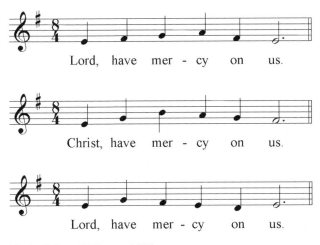

Lord, have mer - cy on us.

Christ, have mer - cy on us.

Lord, have mer - cy on us.

Music: F. Russell Mitman, 2005

All: **Our Father in heaven,**
hallowed be your name,
your kingdom come,
your will be done,
on earth as in heaven.
Give us today our daily bread.
Forgive us our sins
as we forgive those who sin against us.
Save us from the time of trial
and deliver us from evil.
For the kingdom, the power, and the glory are yours
now and forever. Amen.

An optional hymn or Psalm may be sung or spoken.

Leader: Go forth into this day with Christ's promise and blessing:
"Peace I leave with you, peace such as the world cannot give.
Let not your hearts be troubled, neither let them be afraid.
I am the vine, and you are the branches;
abide in my love that my joy may be in you, and your joy complete."
—John 14:27; 15:5, 9, 11, adapt.

All: **Praise and thanks to you, O Christ. Alleluia!**

Chapter Three

Evening Prayer

The practice of gathering for evening prayer has its origins in the earliest times of the Christian church, perhaps even as a continuation of practices in Judaism, allusions to which appear in Psalm 141:1–2. Depending on the tradition during the Christian patristic era, evening prayers took the form of either late-afternoon prayers when natural light was waning and candles were lighted (vespers) or night prayers (matins) that were anticipatory of the dawn and were shaped by the great Easter vigil. And between the two there developed the practice of prayer at the end of the day (compline) before going to sleep. Eventually, during the monastic period, these got incorporated into the daily prayer practices surrounding the observance of the seven canonical hours that later became canonized in the Roman Breviary. All of them focused on the recitation or chanting of Psalms and other canticles.

Although these evening prayers were intended to be corporate worship acts for which the whole community gathered, there are few remnants left, except for midweek services during Lent, in most of mainline American Protestantism. Many denominational worship books and hymnals include services for evening prayer, yet the scheduling of communal prayer in the evening in most churches is sporadic at best. We seem to want a full dose on Sunday mornings, but we leave daily prayers to individual piety, most often to quick prayers before meals, and to our children ("Now I lay me down to sleep . . .") at bedtime before the kids outgrow the habit! However, with more congregations scheduling alternative worship times and services, it may be helpful for churches to revive the opportunity for evening prayer, not as just one more preaching service or Bible study but as a time for repetitive prayers and chants that enable people to be immersed in a larger reality than that which has consumed most of their day's occupation.

Evening prayer provides opportunities for assemblies to experience many of the nonverbal worship expressions that perhaps they would not tolerate in other settings. Many congregations already are accustomed to lighting candles on Christmas Eve and, less frequently, in Tenebrae services on Maundy Thursday or Good Friday. Many families light candles to create an intimate atmosphere for dining in the home, and the use of incense and other aromas are increasingly welcomed, even as therapy. For some strange reason, some people seem more ready to exchange expressions of peace, even embraces, in the evening than as a gathering expression at the beginning of worship in the morning. Evening prayer, when darkness falls, becomes a time to experience the intimacy of God and of the community who gather to bless God and to be blessed somewhere toward the end of the day. A service of evening prayer may provide a fitting conclusion to a church meeting or small group study gathering.

Traditionally services of evening prayer include a setting of the Magnificat, the prayer, according to Luke, that Mary prayed following the divine disclosure that she would bear the Christ. There are a variety of wonderful musical settings of this Scripture passage that may be used. Suggestions are: "My Heart Sings Out with Joyful Praise" by Ruth Duck, "Surely It Is God Who Saves Me" by Carl P. Daw Jr., and "My Soul Gives Glory to My God" by Miriam Therese Winter. An alternative is the prayer paraphrase of Luke 2:46–55 that is included in this text. The Kyrie and the Trisagion — ancient worship expressions that originated in the earliest Christian traditions — are included in new musical forms that I have composed.

It is important that very few verbal instructions be given. This liturgy is intended to be used in like manner on each occasion so that the assembly does not get "hung up" on frequent changes and so that the focus is not on the leader but on God, who is the subject of the worship. Everything that is necessary for the assembly's participation should be printed in a worship folder or bulletin. This liturgy can be copied and adapted for each congregation's use from the accompanying CD-ROM and, with proper acknowledgment, may be reproduced in sufficient quantity for each observance. Keyboard accompaniments for the Response to Psalm 16, the Kyrie, and the Trisagion, may be found on pages 171 and 172.

A LITURGY FOR EVENING PRAYER
CD-ROM 3.1.1

Each person upon entering the worship space may be given an unlighted candle. A bell or bells may be rung. All may stand.

Leader: Come, bless the Lord, all you servants of the Lord,
who stand by night in the house of the Lord!
Lift up your hands to the holy place,
and bless the Lord.   —Psalm 134:1–2

All: **Stay with us, Lord, because it is almost evening
and the day is now nearly over.**   —Luke 24:29, adapt.

An acolyte may carry a lighted candle into the midst of the assembly or light candles that may be in their customary places. As the acolyte lights the candle(s), the leader continues:

Leader: Jesus said,
"I am the light of the world.
Whoever follows me will never walk in darkness
but will have the light of life."   —John 8:12

All: **Let the light of your face shine on us, O Lord!**   —Psalm 4:6b

The leader may light a taper from a candle and distribute the light to several people who, in turn, pass the light to others. Those receiving the light should dip their candles to the ones already lit. Do not dip a lighted candle. After all candles are lit, the leader continues:

Leader: It is good to give thanks to the Lord,

All: **to sing praises to your name, O Most High;**

Leader: to declare your steadfast love in the morning,

All: **and your faithfulness by night.**   —Psalm 92:1–2

The assembly may speak the following prayer or sing it in unison or, repeated several times, as a round.

> **All praise to you, my God, this night,**   TALLIS CANON
> **for all the blessings of the light!**
> **Keep me, as night falls, safe from harm,**
> **within the shadow of your arm.**
>
> Words: Thomas Ken, 1692, alt.

The assembly is seated. A period of silence is observed.

Leader: I call upon you, O Lord; come quickly to me;

All: **give ear to my voice when I call to you.**

A pot of burning incense may be brought to the place where prayers will be offered.

Leader: Let my prayer be counted as incense before you,

All: **and the lifting up of my hands as an evening sacrifice.** —Psalm 141:1–2

All may lift up hands as the leader prays:

Leader: We lift up our hands to you, O God,
                 and we offer all that has been part of this day to you:
                 the good and the bad, the fulfilling and the frustrating,
                 the times we have honored you and affirmed others,
                 the times we have disobeyed you and harmed others.
                 To you we lift up all we have thought and said and done,
                 asking you to forgive us when we have missed the mark
                 of your intentions for us,
                 and to bless us when, in our finite and human ways,
                 we have accomplished what you have wanted us to do;
                 Through Jesus Christ, our Lord.

All: **Amen.**

The assembly may speak or sing the following adaptation of Psalm 16.

Response:

Pro - tect   me,   O   God,   for   in   you   I   take   re - fuge.

Leader: Protect me, O God, for in you I take refuge.

All: **I say to the Lord, "You are my Lord;**
                 I have no good apart from you." *Response*

Leader: The Lord is my chosen portion and my cup.

All: **The boundary lines have fallen for me in pleasant places;**
                 I have a goodly heritage.

Leader: I bless the Lord who gives me counsel;
                 in the night also my heart instructs me.

All: **I keep the Lord always before me;**
                 because God is at my right hand,
                 I shall not be moved. *Response*

Leader: Therefore my heart is glad, and my soul rejoices;

All: **my body also rests secure.**

Leader: You show me the path of life.

**All: In your presence there is fullness of joy;
            in your right hand are pleasures forevermore.** *Response*

Words: Psalm 16:1–2, 5–9, 11, adapt.; Music: F. Russell Mitman, 2005

Leader: Listen for the Word of God in a reading from _____.

One or more passages of Scripture are read, each followed by:

Leader: The Word of the Lord.

All: Thanks be to God.

Silence or a brief homily may follow.

The assembly may sing a musical setting of the Magnificat (Canticle of Mary) or pray in unison the following paraphrase:

Leader: Let us pray to God as Mary prayed:

**All: My soul magnifies the Lord,
            and my spirit rejoices in God my Savior,
            for you have looked with favor on the lowliness of your servant.
            Surely, from now on all generations will call me blessed;
            for you, the Mighty One, have done great things for me,
            and holy is you name.
            Your mercy is for those who fear you
            from generation to generation.
            You have shown strength with your arm,
            and have scattered the proud in the thoughts of their hearts.
            You have brought down the powerful from their thrones,
            filled the hungry with good things,
            and sent the rich away empty.
            You have helped your servant Israel,
            in remembrance of your mercy,
            according to the promise you made to our ancestors,
            to Abraham and to his descendants forever.**
                                            — Luke 2:46–55, paraphrased

Leader: The Lord be with you.

All: And also with you.

Leader: That you will forgive whatever we have done this day
            to you and to others
            that has not been acceptable and well-pleasing in your sight
            and that may have brought pain to others,

All: *singing or speaking*

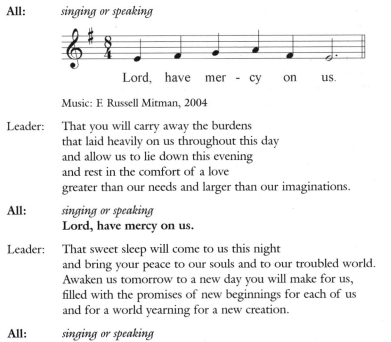

Lord, have mer - cy on us.

Music: F. Russell Mitman, 2004

Leader: That you will carry away the burdens
that laid heavily on us throughout this day
and allow us to lie down this evening
and rest in the comfort of a love
greater than our needs and larger than our imaginations.

All: *singing or speaking*
Lord, have mercy on us.

Leader: That sweet sleep will come to us this night
and bring your peace to our souls and to our troubled world.
Awaken us tomorrow to a new day you will make for us,
filled with the promises of new beginnings for each of us
and for a world yearning for a new creation.

All: *singing or speaking*
Lord, have mercy on us.

Other intercessions may be offered, followed by silence.

Leader: Hear our prayers, O Lord;

All: **give ear to my supplications in your faithfulness;**
answer me in your righteousness. —Psalm 143:1–2, adapt.

The following may be said or sung.

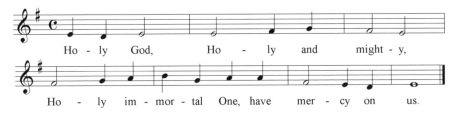

Ho - ly God, Ho - ly and might - y,
Ho - ly im - mor - tal One, have mer - cy on us.

Words: *Trisagion* c. 434 AD; Music: F. Russell Mitman, 2005

All: **Our Father in heaven,**
hallowed be your name,
your kingdom come,
your will be done,
on earth as in heaven.

Give us today our daily bread.
Forgive us our sins
as we forgive those who sin against us.
Save us from the time of trial
and deliver us from evil.
For the kingdom, the power, and the glory are yours
now and forever. Amen.

An optional hymn or Psalm may be sung or spoken.

Leader: Listen to the comforting assurance of the grace of God,
           promised in the Gospel of our Lord Jesus Christ:
           "Peace I leave with you; my peace I give to you.
           I do not give to you as the world gives.
           Do not let your hearts be troubled,
           and do not let them be afraid."   —John 14:27

All: **Amen.**

Leader: May the peace of God that surpasses all understanding,
           guard your hearts and your minds in Christ Jesus.

                                                    —Philippians 4:7, adapt.

All: **Amen.**

Candles may be extinguished, and the assembly may exchange expressions of peace.

Chapter Four

Penitence and Forgiveness

Including:

*A Liturgy for Corporate or Individual Penitence
with an Alternative Setting for Ash Wednesday*

A Liturgy for Eucharist on Ash Wednesday

In the church of my childhood holy communion was an occasional service that was celebrated four times a year. There was a separate liturgy for these services that found a special place in the hymnal not as part of, but in addition to, the order for the "regular" Sunday service. The renewal in worship that took place in most mainline churches in the latter half of the twentieth century corrected that liturgical aberration and provided for one common service in which the celebration of the Eucharist is normative but provides for an alternative ending following the offertory on those occasions when the Eucharist is not celebrated.

Another occasional service in that hymnal was called the "Preparatory Service," which also replaced the "regular" Sunday service on the Sundays before the quarterly communions. In essence it was an order for penitence and forgiveness to prepare worshipers for what would take place the next time they gathered. The order began with the minister reading the Ten Commandments and Christ's summary of the Law followed by a brief prayer that these would be "written in our hearts." What I remember so vividly is what followed — a lengthy litany of repentance and intercession, adapted from the Great Litany of the *Book of Common Prayer,* for which the assembly was directed to kneel. Although the sanctuary did not include kneelers, the assembly kneeled on the floor backward, facing the back of the pews and propping their elbows on the uncushioned seats of the pews. Even though I counted the number of times the liturgy called for "Good Lord, deliver us," obviously the remembrance of the prayer posture engraved itself in my memory. It was made clear to us — even

47

without verbal rubrics — that we were about a serious confession of sins that included the pastor petitioning, among other things, "from sedition and rebellion; from heresy and schism; from hardness of heart and contempt of thy Word and authority," and the assembly responding, "Good Lord, deliver us." Yet that was not the end. Following the sermon there was a lengthy exhortation by the minister about the sacredness of the holy communion and a warning about not coming to the table without repentance — and the sure consequences of impenitence. Then there was another lengthy confession of sin — for which everyone again was enjoined to kneel backward — followed by confessional questions that were asked by the minister, to which the assembly dutifully responded, "I do." Finally, at the end of the service there was an assurance of pardon, a doxology, and a final benediction. This was a full-blown rite of penance — albeit corporate — in which the sins of the penitents, their forebears, and their society were clearly defined, and of which the minister asked, "Do you repent?" These sins were pardoned not by priestly authority but by the promise of John 3:16 and the promise of the penitents to lead lives of faith. The megachurch movement and cultural Protestantism have eliminated such harshnesses — verbal and nonverbal — because "nice people" shouldn't be subjected to such negativity and asked to say such terrible things. Obviously, such services would have few in attendance today.

Yet there is something that stirs in the souls of many, an unsettledness that not all is well with one's soul and the soul of society, a sometimes almost unconscious awareness that somehow we've missed the mark God intends for us. What gets translated as "sin" from the New Testament Greek is *hamartia,* and this has its origin in military practice. *Hamartia* is what happens when the archer aims at the target, draws the bow, and lets the arrow fly, yet the arrow misses the target. Despite the denial mechanisms our culture lures us to buy, there is still an underlying perception that somehow, in the words of the ancient prayer book that sometimes get left out of modern redactions: "there is no health in us." And the only way there can be healing is for there to be some spiritual discipline that allows the missing-of-the-mark to come to consciousness, to be acknowledged and confessed, and then for us to receive pardon and forgiveness. It is said that "confession is good for the soul," yes, but more than confession alone is the need to be forgiven, forgiven by God but also forgiven by other human beings who may have been wronged by the ways in which we have missed the mark of what human relationships are meant to be, and likewise the need to forgive those who have sinned against us. In contemporary society so often there is talk in the public arena of "justice" — when a crime has been committed or when a nation seeks to justify its invasion of another nation. Actually what is at stake is not justice but retaliation, that is, one perpetration supposedly justifies a retaliatory response. Penitence and forgiveness, however, are at polar opposites of revenge and retaliation. To come to the posture of penitence and to receive and to give forgiveness are acknowledgments of human vulnerability and accountability before God and others in the human community. Without opportunities for penitence and forgiveness — both individual and corporate — our liturgies are less than complete, and our lives are less than whole.

In contemporary Lutheran and Anglican liturgies there are brief orders of public confession that precede the service of Word and Sacrament. (The post–Vatican II order for the mass in the Roman Catholic Church also offers such an introductory penitential rite as an alternative to the blessing of the water.) These may be separate acts or serve as introductory rites to services of Word and Sacrament in which the gathering rites begin with Kyrie and Gloria in Excelsis. In most services of Word and Sacrament in the Reformed tradition, an act of public confession of sin is part of the gathering itself, and often the Kyrie is folded into a penitential portion of the gathering or becomes part of a separate penitential act that either precedes the reading of Scripture and preaching or, in some cases, *follows* Scripture and sermon as a response to the Word of God. The latter is also the case in the rites for Eucharist in the *Book of Common Prayer* used by churches in the Protestant Episcopal tradition and others. In liturgies of the Reformed tradition frequently the Gloria in Excelsis is seen as a doxological response to receiving the words of forgiveness that follow the confession of sin. Hence, there is general ecumenical consensus that a public rite of confession of sin is an integral part of the normative liturgies for the celebration of Word and Sacrament.

There is another occasion for which there has been a traditional rite of penitence and forgiveness, namely, the observance of Ash Wednesday. This day, which marks the beginning of the forty-day Lenten period, is named for a traditional act of placing ashes on foreheads as a sign of penitence and contrition. In essence, the liturgies that have been shaped by the Ash Wednesday experience are services of corporate penitence and forgiveness. The imposition of ashes is a nonverbal symbol that reinforces the penitential act and serves as a visual and tactile reminder of our own humanity and mortality as we begin the forty-day walk with the one who emptied himself and took upon himself the form of a slave. Although the imposition of ashes may seem a bit foreign to many mainline Protestants, there is a growing acceptance of this rite in some churches. People are beginning to appreciate the rich meaning this simple act communicates and find it a way of experiencing God's blessing in ways beyond mere words.

This service, with its alternate prayer of confession and with or without the imposition of ashes, may be used as the beginning of an Ash Wednesday service. If so, then the service following this act continues with the reading of Scriptures and a homily or sermon, followed by prayers of intercession and the Eucharist. A simple liturgy for Eucharist that complements the Ash Wednesday settings of this service may be found on page 57.

All of the above are settings for *corporate* penitence and forgiveness. Although there is a common convergence about the place of confession in liturgical practice, there is divergence, however, regarding *individual* penitential rites. By the time of the Reformation of the sixteenth century and the Roman Catholic reaction in the Council of Trent, penance had become one of the seven sacraments of the Roman Catholic Church. Because of abuses, particularly regarding the sale of indulgences, that had occurred surrounding the practice and usage of penance, most of the Reformers generally abandoned private confessions. Luther, however, said:

> Of private confession, which is now observed, I am hearty in favor, even though it cannot be proved from the Scriptures; it is useful and necessary, nor would I have it abolished — no, I rejoice that it exists in the Church of Christ, for it is a cure without an equal for distressed consciences. (*The Babylonian Captivity of the Church*, 4.13)

Calvin affirmed that the fundamental sacrament of forgiveness is baptism in which the person is engrafted into Christ and is given, out of God's sheer grace, the continual forgiveness of sin. Hence Calvin stressed that liturgies of confession should not only focus on the sin and the sinner but also on the forgiveness and grace of the God who forgives sin. Whereas the medieval practice of penance focused on the "satisfaction," that is, what the sinner would be required to do as a consequence of confession and absolution, both Luther and Calvin believed such acts of works righteousness to be abhorrent and in violation of Scripture. The only satisfaction that can be made to God, Luther affirmed, is by the faith of a contrite heart.

However, Luther's awareness that perhaps private confession could help "distressed consciences" may invite us to revisit this liturgical practice today. The pastoral care movement that captivated the church in the latter decades of the twentieth century sought to align in a more disciplined way the insights of the psychotherapeutic community with the care that pastors have been known to give as part of the pastoral office. It is clear that a form of private confession has taken place in many pastors' studies and therapists' offices. There is a deep desire on the part of some in the faith community to see their path of healing as part of their religious pilgrimage. And even among those who do not seek therapeutic intervention, there is a need to confess and to receive forgiveness for what they believe cannot be said corporately. The liturgical practice of penitence and forgiveness can be an integral part of the whole church's ministry of pastoral care and reconciliation. This is not restricted to the "professional" role of pastors. By the baptismal commissioning of the priesthood of all the believers, there is also a spiritual authority given to all the baptized to forgive sins in the name of Jesus Christ. And those who confess need to hear the good news that they are forgiven; a transformational release — a blessing — occurs that is truly a sign of the working of the Holy Spirit when a person hears and acknowledges that he or she is forgiven.

Therefore, the liturgy included here can be used both in corporate worship as well as on occasions of individual penitence and forgiveness. It can serve as a more than brief order of public confession that shapes the gathering and penitential acts in services of Word and Sacrament. It can become the prelude to a service of healing or to a penitential service that may be occasioned by some national or international calamity. And, adapted, it can serve as a liturgy of individual penitence and forgiveness. Care needs to be given in private confession, as in any one-to-one relationship of pastoral care, that strict ethical boundaries between both the one hearing the confession and the one making the confession are maintained. The place of confession needs to be a place of confidentiality and yet within a building in which others are present. There may be occasions when married couples or families seek reconciliation and the need for some liturgical act of penitence and forgiveness that becomes for them a sign of blessing.

Worship folders or bulletins for participants, including occasions of individual penitence, need to be prepared. This liturgy appears on the accompanying CD-ROM, and whoever is preparing the worship folders or bulletins may adapt the liturgy for a corporate or individual act of penitence and forgiveness.

A musical setting of Psalm 130 is included. This Psalm also may be spoken responsively, particularly when this liturgy is used for individual or small-group penitence and forgiveness. The music for the cantor and the keyboard accompaniment may be found on page 173 and may be copied from the accompanying CD-ROM. If the Psalm is spoken, the leader may assume the cantor's role, and the final two petitions of the choir and cantor are eliminated. Also, a musical setting of the Trisagion is optional. A four-part setting, which also may serve as a keyboard accompaniment, may be found on page 172 and may be copied for choir or quartet from the accompanying CD-ROM.

A LITURGY FOR
CORPORATE OR INDIVIDUAL PENITENCE
WITH AN ALTERNATIVE SETTING
FOR ASH WEDNESDAY
CD-ROM 4.1.1

For Corporate Penitence

Leader: Our worship is in the Name of the Triune God.

A hymn may be sung.
The leader may pour water into the font and say:

Leader: Remember your baptism and give thanks!

All: Amen.

The leader may invite those who desire to dip their fingers into the water and to make the sign of the cross on their foreheads or on the foreheads of others and to say to each other: "Remember your baptism and give thanks!" The individual response may be: "Amen."

Or

The leader may pour water into a bowl, dip evergreen branches into the bowl, and sprinkle the water over those assembled. As the sprinkling (asperges) takes place, the leader and assembly may exchange repeatedly: "Remember your baptism and give thanks!" The individual response may be: "Amen."

After either of the above, the leader continues:

Leader: As a deer longs for flowing streams,

All: so my soul longs for you, O God.   — Psalm 42:1

Leader: Our souls yearn for you, O God, for the living God.

All: We have wandered aimlessly trying to find meaning for our lives, yet we are lost and do not know where we are going.

We have insisted on aiming our intentions by our ourselves,
but have missed the mark you intend for us.
So we come emotionally tired and spiritually exhausted,
yearning to find the living water
that once again will drench the dryness of our souls.

Silence

For Ash Wednesday
CD-ROM 4.1.2

If this liturgy is used on Ash Wednesday, the service begins with the following:

Leader: God proves his love for us in that while we still were sinners
Christ died for us. — Romans 5:8

All: **Behold the lamb of God who takes away the sin of the world!**
— John 1:29, RSV

A hymn such as "Before the Cross of Jesus" may be sung.

Leader: If we say we have no sin, we deceive ourselves,
and the truth is not in us.

All: **But if we confess our sins, God who is faithful and just
will forgive our sins and cleanse us from all unrighteousness.**

— 1 John 1:8–9

Leader: Let us pray

All: **Converting God, whose face is turned toward us in Jesus Christ:
we come this *day/night* to be turned:
Turned from the ways, barren and desolate,
on which we have spent our lives,
Turned from the ways of self-gratification that have sold our souls
to the idols and images of a materialistic world,
Turned from the ways of exploitation
that have destroyed our relationships with others
and with the good creation you have given us.
In dust and ashes, we confess our sin
and our complicity in the sins of our society,
and we come to be turned:
Turned to follow the other road that leads to Jerusalem,
to Gethsemane, to Golgotha, and to Joseph's garden,
Turned to follow with Jesus the way of the cross,
that we may share also with Christ
in the new life of resurrection's dawn.**

Silence

For Individual Penitence
CD-ROM 4.1.3

For individual penitence the service begins with the following:

Minister: The grace of our Lord Jesus Christ,
the love of God,
and the communion of the Holy Spirit
be with you.   — 2 Corinthians 13:13

All/One: **And also with you.**

Leader: When we come into the holy presence of God,
our own humanity is laid bare.
When we stand in the living presence of truth,
our own falsehood is revealed.
Let us acknowledge who we are
and ask God to forgive us.

Participants may bow or kneel.

All/One: **O God of new starts and fresh beginnings,**
** *I/we* come to you today**
**   burdened with the past's leftovers.**
** *I/we* feel guilty over the things *I/we* have left unfinished**
**   and the things *I/we* intended to start**
**   but never got around to doing.**
** *I/we* have grieved over life's little losses**
**   but have failed to search for the big finds.**
** *I/we* would rather be obsessed by what has passed *me/us* by**
**   than to rejoice in what lies ahead.**
** Come after *us/me* in *our/my* wanderings, O God,**
**   like a shepherd hunting for a lost sheep,**
**   like a woman sweeping the house for a missing coin.**
** Find *us/me* in *our/my* lostness,**
**   and wrap *us/me* in an extravagant grace**
**   that lifts *us/me* on your shoulders**
**   and takes *us/me* where you want *us/me* to be. Amen.**

Silence

All Settings

In all settings the service continues:

Leader: Is there anything you wish to confess before God,
either aloud or in silence?

Silence

Psalm 130 may be spoken responsively or sung to the following tune:

Cantor: Out of the depths I cry to you, O Lord.

All:

Cantor: Let your ears be attentive to the voice of my supplications!

All: **Lord, hear my voice!**

Cantor: If you, O Lord, should mark iniquities, Lord, who could stand?

All: **Lord, hear my voice!**

Cantor: But there is forgiveness with you, so that you may be revered.

All: **Lord, hear my voice!**

Cantor: I wait for the Lord, my soul waits, and in God's word do I hope.

All: **Lord, hear my voice!**

Cantor: My soul waits for the Lord
more than those who watch for the morning,
more than those who watch for the morning.

All: **Lord, hear my voice!**

Cantor: O Israel, hope in the Lord! For with the Lord there is steadfast love,
and with God is great power to redeem.

All: **Lord, hear my voice!**

Choir: Lord, hear my voice!

Cantor: Lord, hear my voice!

Words: Psalm 130:1–7, alt.; Music: F. Russell Mitman, 2005

The following confessional questions may be asked:

Leader: In the presence of God, I ask you,
Do you acknowledge that your have missed the mark
God intends for you?

All/One: **I do.**

Leader: Do you believe that God is willing, for Jesus' sake,
to forgive all your sins?

All/One: **I do.**

Leader: Do you resolve to allow the Holy Spirit to direct you,
           so that you may forgive others as God has forgiven you?

All/One: I do.

The following may be sung or spoken:

> **Lord, have mercy on us.**
> **Christ, have mercy on us.**
> **Lord, have mercy on us.**

Or:

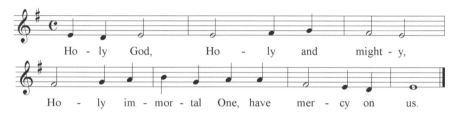

Words: *Trisagion* c. 434 AD; Music: F. Russell Mitman, 2005

Silence

If this liturgy is used for an Ash Wednesday observance, and if ashes are to be imposed, the leader lifts the container of ashes and prays:

Leader: Creator God who fashioned us from the dust of the earth,
           bless these ashes that they may be a sign of our mortality,
           and a reminder of your forgiving grace
           through the death and resurrection of your Son,
           Jesus Christ, our Lord. Amen.

Those who desire may come to a place where ashes are to be imposed. A hymn may be sung, or silence may be kept. The leader dips his or her thumb into the ashes and makes a sign of the cross on the forehead of each person with the following words:

Leader: Remember that you are dust,
           and to dust you shall return.

In all settings the service continues, the leader standing at the font:

Leader: Listen to the comforting assurance of the grace of God,
           promised in the Gospel to all who repent and believe:

> God so loved the world that he gave his only Son,
> so that everyone who believes in him
> may not perish but may have eternal life.

Indeed, God did not send the Son into the world to condemn the world, but in order that the world might be saved through him.

—John 3:16–17

Believe the Good news!
In Jesus Christ *your/our* sins are forgiven!

All: **Amen. Thanks be to God!**

The hymn "Amazing Grace" may be sung.

Minister: Let us give one another a sign of our reconciliation in Christ.

All may greet one another and/or exchange the Peace of Christ.

The service may end with a doxology or hymn. If this liturgy is a preface to a service of Word and Sacrament, the service continues with the reading of Scriptures and a sermon or homily.

A LITURGY FOR EUCHARIST
ON ASH WEDNESDAY
CD-ROM 4.2.1

This order begins following the offering. The elements may be brought to the altar/table during the singing of the hymn verses. The doxology in the Eucharistic prayer is adapted from an old German table grace. It may be sung or said responsively or in unison.

Minister: Let us approach the table of our Lord
                  in true penitence and contrition.

All: *singing; the assembly remains seated.*

ST. FLAVIAN

Lord Jesus, who through forty days for us did fast and pray,
Teach us with you to mourn our sins, and close by you to stay.

As you with Satan did contend and did the victory win,
O give us strength to persevere, in you to conquer sin.

Words: Claudia F. I. Hernaman, 1873, alt.

Minister: Lift up your hearts!

All: **We lift them up to the Lord!**

The congregation may stand.

Minister: Let us give thanks:

All: **It is right to give God thanks and praise!**

Minister: For your creating hand that brought the worlds into being
and fashions every living thing,
and for stretching your holy arm
to bring your people in every generation from bondage to freedom:

All: **Receive our thanks, O God.**

Minister: For coming to us in Jesus our Lord,
sharing our human lot, suffering and dying for us,
and being raised that we, too, may share in resurrection life:

All: **Receive our praise, O God.**

Minister: For the outpouring of your Holy Spirit,
calling and empowering the church
with an abundance of spiritual gifts:

All: **Receive, O God, our offering of thanksgiving and praise.**

Spoken antiphonally or sung in unison to OLD HUNDREDTH:

Minister: Be present at our table, Lord!

All: **Be here and everywhere adored!**

Minister: Bless now this bread and wine we share,

All: **And for heaven's banquet us prepare.**

Minister: *breaking the bread*
The Lord Jesus on the night when he was betrayed took bread,
and when he had given thanks, he broke it, and said,
"This is my body which is given for you.
Do this in remembrance of me."

pouring the cup
In the same way he also took the cup, after supper, saying,
"This cup is the new covenant in my blood.
Do this, as often as you drink it, in remembrance of me."

Minister: Behold the Lamb of God who takes away the sin of the world!

All: **Our Father...**

*During the distribution, the minister or reader(s) may read without references Isaiah 53:4–6
and John 4:9–11.*

Minister: For broken bread and outpoured wine,
signs of your life given and spilled out in love
for us and for all humankind, we give you thanks, O Christ.

All: *singing*   ST. FLAVIAN

Lord, through these days of penitence, and through your Passiontide,
Yes, evermore, in life and death, Jesus, with us abide.

Abide with us, that so, this life of suffering over-past
An Easter of unending joy we may attain at last!

Words: Claudia F. I. Hernaman, 1873, alt.

Chapter Five

Washing

Including:

*A Liturgy of Washing for Maundy Thursday
and Other Penitential Occasions*

*A Liturgy for Maundy Thursday Eucharist
Including Tenebrae*

Ecumenical work in the area of liturgical renewal in recent years has led to the recovery of some worship practices that, for any number of reasons, were abandoned or forgotten in previous centuries of the church's life. Some of these liturgies, particularly three that together are called the *triduum,* or "three days" (Maundy Thursday, Good Friday, and the Great Vigil), trace their origins to earliest Christianity. Over the centuries the intrinsic unity of the three days' liturgies was lost as individual rites and celebrations were lifted out of their total context or were abandoned for theological and cultural reasons.

One ancient rite that was clearly a practice of the early Christian community as witnessed to in the Gospel of John (John 13:1–20) is footwashing. John's account of Jesus' Passover meal does not include the institution of communion found in the Synoptic Gospels. Instead, "during supper," John says, "Jesus . . . got up from the table, took off his outer robe, and tied a towel around himself. Then he poured water into a basin and began to wash the disciples' feet and to wipe them with the towel" (John 13:2a–5). Clearly John's focus here is not so much on the meal itself as on Jesus' servant role and the injunction to the church: "So if I, your Lord and Teacher, have washed your feet, you also ought to wash one another's feet. For I have set you an example, that you also should do as I have done to you" (John 13:14–15).

There have been discussions both in history and in contemporary conversations as to whether this injunction is the institution of an ordinance or simply a symbol of how those who would follow Jesus should be servants to one another. The remembrance of this biblical story is preserved in the Roman Catholic tradition in which the pope on Maundy Thursday washes the feet of twelve men, presuming that Jesus washed the feet of twelve male disciples. The rite is continued in Roman Catholic parishes and some other hierarchical churches in which the priest, as the representative of Christ, washes the feet of twelve people — symbolizing a reversal of the servant role. Mennonites and some other Anabaptist churches have preserved footwashing as an ordinance in which the members of the community wash each other's feet in preparation for the communal love feast. In these settings the footwashings may occur at times other than on Maundy Thursday.

Most of the so-called mainline Protestant communities simply abandoned the practice, most often, I believe, for cultural reasons. The theological justification sometimes given for not physically washing other people's feet is that this simply was a cultural practice of people who lived in the dry and dusty climates of the Middle East and wore sandals as their everyday footwear. It is argued that in present-day European and American settings where footwear, in a sense, privatizes people's feet and some people have deep sensitivity about exposing their feet or touching someone else's feet, the story of Jesus' washing his disciples' feet should be read and heard for its message about humility and servanthood, but not be practiced liturgically. However, there are some of us in mainline Protestant traditions who believe that the liturgical recovery of this ancient rite is important for Christians — not just to dramatize an event that the writer of the Gospel of John tells us Jesus did, but as a liturgical act for the church today. The official books of worship of several mainline churches now include footwashing as part of their Maundy Thursday liturgies. In a culture that rewards power and avoids whatever exposes human vulnerability, footwashing can become a means of grace individually and corporately for the living of these days.

I have titled this discussion "Washing," rather than "footwashing," because there can be, I believe, alternative modes of administering this rite. Handwashing, although it misses the sense of allowing oneself to be subservient to another person as in footwashing, still preserves the opportunity for corporate confession and the nonverbal communication that takes place when people touch each other in the act of wiping the other's hands with the towel. For those congregations to whom the whole idea is very foreign, handwashing may be a step along the journey that could eventuate in footwashing itself. Hence, I have provided for the alternative mode of administration in the accompanying liturgy.

Although there is scriptural warrant for this act in the same way in which the church has looked to the accounts in the Synoptic Gospels and Paul's first letter to the Corinthians as Jesus' institution of the Lord's Supper, I do not wish to engage in the lengthy and sometimes circular debate over the difference between sacraments and rites. Nevertheless, I invite participants, through actions sometimes more powerful than words, to experience for themselves this simple act that exposes our human vulnerability and that can become a means of being washed and touched by God's extraordinary grace.

In the Middle Ages civil authority frequently was joined with the ecclesiastical rites of the church. Persons who had committed civil crimes throughout the year — and thus were excommunicated from the church — were given the opportunity for confession in the Maundy Thursday rite so that they could be restored to communion on Easter. This liturgy includes the act of corporate confession. The prayer in this liturgy is an adaptation of Psalm 51 in which the pronouns in the leader's readings are pluralized as corporate petitions while the pronouns in the congregation's lines are kept in the singular as individual confessions. And folks may kneel if they so desire! The sounds and sights of water being poured and the *asperges*, that is, sprinkling the congregation with water, are nonverbal reminders of the waters of baptism and preludes to the washing rite.

The washing liturgy is shaped by the account of Jesus' washing his disciples feet in John 13:1ff., which is the appointed Gospel lesson in the *Revised Common Lectionary* each year for Maundy Thursday. Although the footwashing account in Scripture is high drama, this liturgy does not intend to be a dramatic performance or a passion play that tries to show what John tells us Jesus did with his disciples before his death and resurrection. Rather, it sees what is recorded in Scripture through the eyes of faith, through the resurrection community. We see the events at the end of Jesus' life from the other side of betrayal and death, *after* Easter, through the lens of Jesus' resurrection and ascension, and through the life of the church after Pentecost. It is enacted today as a sign-act and means of grace for the church for "the living of *these* days."

This order attempts to take seriously Jesus' injunction according to John: "You also ought to wash one another's feet. For I have set you an example, that you also should do as I have done to you" (John 13:14b–15). The rubrics call for a communal participation in which each person is priest to another person. Although footwashing traditionally is seen as a

Maundy Thursday observance, this liturgy of washing can be used in any setting and at any time in which the community of faith seeks literally to be immersed in an act of spiritual cleansing and baptismal remembrance.

The rite of washing may be done best in a place other than in the sanctuary. The observance necessitates certain everyday equipment: basins, pitchers, buckets of fresh water, buckets in which to dispose the wash-water, and plenty of towels. It involves a number of liturgical ministers — with no distinction between "lay" and "clergy." It requires significant re-hearsal so that each feels confident in his or her role. This rite cannot be done with five minutes of verbal instructions. Each person needs to prac-tice his or her part, and the whole needs to be rehearsed so that there is a sense of ensemble among all the leaders. No choir wants to sing without plenty of rehearsal, and, likewise, no one assisting in this liturgy should be expected to do so without rehearsal — and that includes the readers of the Scripture passages.

This liturgy for washing can serve as the bridge between the service of the Word and the Eucharist. If the service through the washing occurs in a room other than the sanctuary, there may be a procession from that room to the sanctuary for the Eucharist. If this liturgy is used on Maundy Thurs-day, I have included a service for Eucharist that is shaped by the upper room experience in Matthew's Gospel and concludes with Matthew's ver-sion of the Passion account. The narration of institution is joined with the breaking of the bread and the pouring of the cup in the hymn "It Happened on That Dreadful Night" by Isaac Watts. Note that the tune MAUNDY shifts from a minor to a major key in the last stanza. The *anam-nesis* (remembrance) of the Eucharistic prayer actually occurs *after* the communion in the Passion narrative. Even though there is violence and shouting in the text, placed where it is in this liturgy, it actually is a way of praying the Scriptures. Although this narration of the Passion is not in-tended to be a substitute for the second day (Good Friday) of the *triduum* observances, it serves in some communities to proclaim in a prayer mode the Good Friday story to members of congregations who want to jump to Easter Sunday and absent themselves from Friday's suffering and death. Even though the *Revised Common Lectionary* now includes the Synoptic passion accounts for each of the three years' observances of Palm/Passion Sunday, there is no harm in including another setting of that story on Maundy Thursday. The prayer of *epiclesis* (to bless the elements) may be spoken by the leader and the assembly as printed or sung in unison to the tune BERTHIER by Jacques Berthier of the Taizé community. I suggest that the Taizé version of "Eat This Bread, Drink This Cup" be sung during the distribution of the elements to tie together musically the prayer of blessing and the giving of the bread and wine.

In some churches Maundy Thursday Eucharist is followed by the rite of Tenebrae ("shadows") in which Scripture readings, prayers, and hymns are sung. Candles are extinguished, one by one, after each of the readings to symbolize the events in Jesus' life following the Upper Room meal through his crucifixion. In the liturgy included here, there are twelve periods of silence that punctuate the Passion narrative. During each of these periods of silence a candle may be extinguished and the lights dimmed. By the last reading, "From noon on, darkness...a Son of God," the room is in darkness. A person stands by each candle, and, following each of the readings, extinguishes that candle and exits. After the twelfth candle is extinguished, only Leader 1 remains. He or she lights the resurrection candle, prays the brief prayer, "Lord Jesus...," and then exits. In this liturgy the same two leaders who have been Leaders 1 and 2 throughout the rite of washing and the Eucharist are the readers for the Passion narrative. Visually and verbally these two leaders tie the three parts of the service together. The role of the twelve at the candles is simply to serve as acolytes to extinguish the candles and, by their exit, to symbolize the gradual desertion of those close to Jesus in his final hours.

The keyboard accompaniments for the tune MAUNDY, both for the first four stanzas in the key of F-minor and the final one in F-major, may be found on pages 176 and 177. An alternate tune is BOURBON.

The liturgy for washing also can be used as the conclusion to a service of the Word on occasions other than Maundy Thursday. The rubrics provide directions for either option.

A LITURGY OF WASHING
FOR MAUNDY THURSDAY AND
OTHER PENITENTIAL OCCASIONS
CD-ROM 5.1.1

The liturgy begins following the sermon.

Leader: Let the same mind be in you that was in Christ Jesus:

All: **Christ, though he was in the form of God,**
           did not regard equality with God
           as something to be exploited,
           but emptied himself,
           taking the form of a slave,
           being born in human likeness.
           And being found in human form,
           he humbled himself
           and became obedient to the point of death—
           even death on a cross.

Leader: Therefore God also highly exalted him
           and gave him the name that is above every name,

All: **So that at the name of Jesus every knee should bend,**
           in heaven and on earth and under the earth,
           and every tongue should confess
           that Jesus Christ is Lord, to the glory of God.   —Philippians 2:5–11

Leader: The Lord be with you.

All: **And also with you.**

Leader: Have mercy on us, O God, according to your steadfast love.

All: **According to your abundant mercy, blot out my transgressions.**

Leader: Wash us thoroughly from our iniquity, and cleanse us from our sin.

All: **For I know my transgressions, and my sin is ever before me.**

Leader: Against you, you alone, have we sinned, and done what is evil in your sight,

All: **Indeed, I was born guilty, a sinner when my mother conceived me.**

Leader: You desire truth in the inward being;

All: **therefore teach me wisdom in my secret heart.**

Leader: Purge us with hyssop, and we shall be clean;

All: **wash me, and I shall be purer than snow.**
                                        —Psalm 51:1–4a, 5–7, adapt.

The server pours water from a pitcher into a basin.

Leader: Bless this water, that it may be a sign
          of your cleansing forgiveness.

**All: Bless me with this water, O God,
          that I may be immersed in a grace deeper than my sin.**

Silence

*The leader(s) may dip evergreen branches into the water and sprinkle persons in the assembly.
This sprinkling (asperges) may be accompanied by:*

Leader: *repeating with each sprinkling:*
          Remember your baptism and give thanks.

Each: Amen.

The assembly may sing, accompanied or a cappella, repeated several times:

Words: Ancient Greek; Music: Russian Orthodox tradition

Leader: Create in us a clean heart, O God.

All: And renew a right spirit within me.

Leader: Do not cast us away from your presence,

All: And do not take your holy spirit from me.

Leader: Restore to us the joy of your salvation,

All: And sustain in me a willing spirit.   —Psalm 51:10–12, adapt.

Silence

Leader: Be assured that the grace of our Lord overflows for us
with the faith and love that are in Christ Jesus.
The saying is sure and worthy of full acceptance,
that Christ Jesus came into the world to save sinners.

— 1 Timothy 1:14–15, adapt.

**All: To the Sovereign of the ages, immortal, invisible, the only God,
be honor and glory forever and ever. Amen.**

— 1 Timothy 1:17, adapt.

Or *singing* ST. DENIO
**Immortal, invisible, God only wise,
in light inaccessible hid from our eyes,
most blessed, most glorious, the Ancient of Days,
almighty, victorious, your great name we praise.**

Hymn stanza: Walter C. Smith, 1867, alt.

Reader 1: Now before the festival of the Passover, Jesus knew that his hour had
come to depart from this world. And during supper Jesus, knowing that
he was going to God, got up from the table, took off his outer robe, and
tied a towel around himself. Then he poured water into a basin and began
to wash the disciples' feet and to wipe them with the towel. He came to
Simon Peter, who said to him,

Reader 2: "Lord, are you going to wash my feet?"

Reader 3: "You do not know now what I am doing, but later you will understand."

Reader 2: "You will never wash my feet."

Reader 3: "Unless I wash you, you have no share with me."

Reader 2: "Lord, not my feet only but also my hands and my head!"

Reader 3: "One who has bathed does not need to wash, but is entirely clean."

Reader 1: After he had washed their feet, had put on his robe, and had returned to
the table, he said to them,

Reader 3: "Do you know what I have done to you? You call me Teacher and Lord—
and you are right, for that is what I am. So if I, your Lord and Teacher,
have washed your feet, you also ought to wash one another's feet. For I
have set you an example, that you also should do as I have done to you."

— John 13:1, 3–10, 12–15, adapt.

Footwashing

Reader 2 is seated. Reader 3 places a basin, a pitcher, and a towel at the feet of Reader 2, who places his or her feet in the basin. Reader 3 pours some of the water over the feet of Reader 2, washes them, and dries them with the towel. Reader 3 then pours the washwater from the basin into the separate bucket. Reader 1 is seated, and Reader 2 (whose feet already have been washed) repeats the procedure with Reader 1. Then Reader 1 repeats the action with Reader 3. Other members of the assembly are invited to wash each other's feet in similar fashion, utilizing the same basin or with other pitchers, basins, and towels at similar stations throughout the room.

Handwashing

Reader 3 invites those who desire to come to the basin. He/she pours water over the hands of another person, washes them, and dries them with the towel. This person (whose hands have been washed) then repeats the procedure with the next person until all who desire have had their hands washed. Fresh water is poured at each washing, and the wash water is emptied into the bucket for disposal.

After persons have had their feet or hands washed, they may greet the one who has washed them with an expression of peace. Hymns or Psalms may be sung or recited. The action also may be done in silence. After all have been washed, the service continues:

Leader: The peace of the Lord Jesus Christ be with you all.

All: And also with you.

Or   **Peace be with you.**

The assembly may exchange words and gestures of peace and reconciliation. Persons may make the sign of the cross on the foreheads of others with the words: "Peace be with you."

The service may continue with the singing of "Peace I Leave With You, My Friends," by Ray Repp, or the Taizé chant, "Ubi Charitas," sung repeatedly. The latter is particularly effective if sung as a processional chant as the community moves from a room to the sanctuary for the Eucharist.

If Eucharist is not included, the service continues with intercessions, offering, the Lord's Prayer, and a sending act.

If this order is used on Maundy Thursday and Eucharist is included, the service continues with the following.

A LITURGY FOR
MAUNDY THURSDAY EUCHARIST
INCLUDING TENEBRAE
CD-ROM 5.2.1

Leader 1: On the first day of Unleavened Bread the disciples came to Jesus, saying, "Where do you want us to make the preparations for you to eat the Passover?"

Leader 2: "Go into the city to a certain man, and say to him, 'The Teacher says, My time is near; I will keep the Passover at your house with my disciples.'"

Leader 1: So the disciples did as Jesus had directed them, and they prepared the Passover meal.

The bread and wine may be brought in silence to the altar/table by those who will administer the elements. They may stand around or near the altar/table. After the table has been set, the service continues:

All: *singing*   MAUNDY

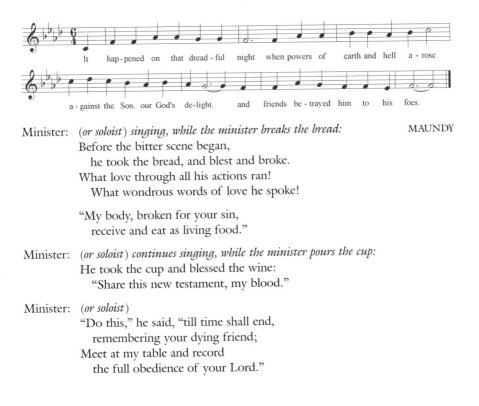

Minister: *(or soloist) singing, while the minister breaks the bread:*   MAUNDY
Before the bitter scene began,
   he took the bread, and blest and broke.
What love through all his actions ran!
   What wondrous words of love he spoke!

"My body, broken for your sin,
   receive and eat as living food."

Minister: *(or soloist) continues singing, while the minister pours the cup:*
He took the cup and blessed the wine:
   "Share this new testament, my blood."

Minister: *(or soloist)*
"Do this," he said, "till time shall end,
   remembering your dying friend;
Meet at my table and record
   the full obedience of your Lord."

All: *singing*   MAUNDY

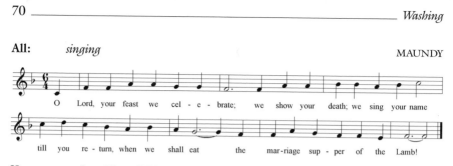

O Lord, your feast we cel - e - brate; we show your death; we sing your name
till you re - turn, when we shall eat the mar-riage sup - per of the Lamb!

Hymn stanzas: Isaac Watts, 1709, alt.; Music: F. Russell Mitman, 2004
Silence

The following prayer may be said as printed or sung in unison to the tune BERTHIER *by Jacques Berthier of the Taizé community.*

Minister: Bless this bread,
            Bless this cup,

All: **Bless us in our eating and drinking.**

Minister: Bless this bread,
            Bless this cup,

All: **Bless all who hunger and thirst.**

Words: F. Russell Mitman, 2005

Intercessions may be offered followed by the Lord's Prayer.

Minister: Come, all things are ready.

During the distribution of the elements:
            Reading or chanting Psalm 116:5–19
            Singing hymns such as "Eat This Bead" (Taizé version)
            and "Go to Dark Gethsemane"

After all have communed, the service continues:

Leader 1:   When they had sung the hymn, they went out to the Mount of Olives.
            Then Jesus said to them,

Leader 2:   "You will all become deserters because of me this night.... But after I am
            raised up, I will go ahead of you to Galilee."

Leader 1:   Peter said to him, "Though all become deserters because of you, I will
            never desert you." Jesus said to him,

Leader 2:   "Truly I tell you, this very night, before the cock crows, you will deny me
            three times."

Leader 1:   Peter said to him, "Even though I must die with you, I will not deny you."
            And so said all the disciples.   —Matthew 26:30–35, adapt.

Silence

Leader 1: Then Jesus went with them to a place called Gethsemane; and he said to his disciples,

Leader 2: "Sit here while I go over there and pray."

Leader 1: He took with him Peter and the two sons of Zebedee, and began to be grieved and agitated. Then he said to them,

Leader 2: "I am deeply grieved, even to death; remain here, and stay awake with me." — Matthew 26:36–38, adapt.

Silence

Leader 1: And going a little farther, he threw himself on the ground and prayed,

Leader 2: "My Father, if it is possible, let this cup pass from me; yet not what I want but what you want." — Matthew 26:39, adapt.

Silence

Leader 1: Then he came to the disciples and found them sleeping; and he said to Peter,

Leader 2: "So could you not stay awake with me one hour? Stay awake and pray that you may not come into the time of trial; the spirit indeed is willing, but the flesh is weak." — Matthew 26:40–41

Silence

Leader 1: Again he went away for the second time and prayed,

Leader 2: "My Father, if this cannot pass unless I drink it, your will be done." — Matthew 26:42, adapt.

Silence

Leader 1: Again he came and found them sleeping, for their eyes were heavy. So leaving them again, he went away and prayed for the third time, saying the same words. Then he came to the disciples and said to them,

Leader 2: "Are you still sleeping and taking your rest? See, the hour is at hand, and the Son of Man is betrayed into the hands of sinners. Get up, let us be going. See, my betrayer is at hand!" — Matthew 26:43–46, adapt.

Silence

Leader 1: While [Jesus] was still speaking, Judas, one of the twelve, arrived; with him was a large crowd with swords and clubs, from the chief priests and the elders of the people. Now the betrayer had given them a sign, saying, "The one I will kiss is the man; arrest him." At once he came up to Jesus and said, "Greetings, Rabbi!" and kissed him.

Leader 2: "Friend, do what you are here to do."

Leader 1: Then they came and laid hands on Jesus and arrested him. Suddenly, one of those with Jesus put his hand on his sword, drew it, and struck the slave of the high priest, cutting off his ear.

Leader 2: "Put you sword back into its place; for all who take the sword will perish by the sword. Do you think that I cannot appeal to my Father and he will at once send me more than twelve legions of angels? But how then would the scriptures be fulfilled, which say it must happen in this way?" . . . "Have you come out with swords and clubs to arrest me as though I were a bandit? Day after day I sat in the temple teaching, and you did not arrest me. But all this has taken place, so that the scriptures of the prophets may be fulfilled."   —Matthew 26:47–56

Silence

Leader 1: Those who had arrested Jesus took him to Caiaphas the high priest, in whose house the scribes and the elders had gathered. But Peter was following him at a distance, as far as the courtyard of the high priest; and going inside, he sat with the guards in order to see how this would end. Now the chief priests and the whole council were looking for false testimony against Jesus so that they might put him to death, but they found none, though many false witnesses came forward. At last two came forward and said, "This fellow said, 'I am able to destroy the temple of God and to build it in three days.'" The high priest stood up and said, "Have you no answer? What is it that they testify against you?" But Jesus was silent. Then the high priest said to him, "I put you under oath before the living God, tell us if you are the Messiah, the Son of God."

Leader 2: "You have said so. But I tell you, from now on you will see the Son of Man seated at the right hand of Power and coming on the clouds of heaven."

Leader 1: Then the high priest tore his clothes and said, "He has blasphemed! Why do we still need witnesses? You have now heard his blasphemy. What is your verdict?" They answered, "He deserves death." Then they spat on his face and struck him, and some slapped him, saying, "Prophesy to us, you Messiah! Who is it that struck you?"   —Matthew 26:57–68

Silence

Leader 1: Now Peter was sitting outside in the courtyard. A servant girl came to him and said, "You also were with Jesus the Galilean." But he denied it before all of them, saying, "I do not know what you are talking about." When he went out to the porch, another servant girl saw him, and she said to the bystanders, "This man was with Jesus of Nazareth." Again he denied it with an oath, "I do not know the man." After a little while the bystanders came up and said to Peter, "Certainly you are also one of them, for your accent betrays you." Then he began to curse and he swore an oath, "I do not know the man!" At that moment the cock crowed. Then Peter remembered what Jesus had said: "Before the cock crows, you will deny me three times." And he went out and wept bitterly.

—Matthew 26:69–75

Silence

Leader 1: When morning came, all the chief priests and the elders of the people conferred together against Jesus in order to bring about his death. They bound him, led him away, and handed him over to Pilate the governor. . . . Jesus stood before the governor; and the governor asked him, "Are you the King of the Jews?"

Leader 2: "You say so."

Leader 1: But when he was accused by the chief priests and elders, he did not answer. Then Pilate said to him, "Do you not hear how many accusations they make against you?" But he gave him no answer, not even to a single charge, so that the governor was greatly amazed.

Leader 1: Now at the festival the governor was accustomed to release a prisoner for the crowd, anyone whom they wanted. At that time they had a notorious prisoner called Jesus Barabbas. So after they had gathered, Pilate said to them, "Whom do you want me to release for you, Jesus Barabbas or Jesus who is called the Messiah?" . . . While he was sitting on the judgment seat, his wife sent word to him, "Have nothing to do with that innocent man, for today I have suffered a great deal because of a dream about him." Now the chief priests and the elders persuaded the crowds to ask for Barabbas and to have Jesus killed. The governor again said to them, "Which of the two do you want me to release for you?"

All: *shouting* **"Barabbas!"**

Leader 1: "Then what should I do with Jesus who is called the Messiah?"

All: *shouting* **"Let him be crucified!"**

Leader 1: "Why, what evil has he done?"

All: *shouting* **"Let him be crucified!"**

Leader 1: So when Pilate saw that he could do nothing, but rather that a riot was beginning, he took some water and washed his hands before the crowd, saying, "I am innocent of this man's blood; see to it yourselves." Then the people as a whole answered,

All: *shouting* **"His blood be on us and on our children!"**

Leader 1: So he released Barabbas for them; and after flogging Jesus, he handed him over to be crucified. —Matthew 27:1–2, 15–26

Silence

Leader 1: Then the soldiers of the governor took Jesus into the governor's headquarters, and they gathered the whole cohort around him. They stripped him and put a scarlet robe on him, and after twisting some thorns into a crown, they put it on his head. They put a reed in his right hand and knelt before him and mocked him, saying, "Hail, King of the Jews!" They spat on him and took the reed and struck him on the head. After mocking him, they stripped him of the robe and put his own clothes on him. Then they led him away to crucify him.   —Matthew 27:27–31

Silence

During this silence the church may be stripped of all appointments — candles, cross, Bible, paraments, linens, and banners. The parament or linen covering the altar/table may be thrown on the floor.

Leader 1: As they went out, they came upon a man from Cyrene named Simon; they compelled this man to carry his cross. And when they came to a place called Golgotha (which means Place of a Skull), they offered him wine to drink, mixed with gall; but when he tasted it, he would not drink it. And when they had crucified him, they divided his clothes among themselves by casting lots; then they sat down there and kept watch over him. Over his head they put the charge against him, which read, "This is Jesus, the King of the Jews."

Then two bandits were crucified with him, one on his right and one on his left. Those who passed by derided him, shaking their heads and saying, "You who would destroy the temple and build it in three days, save yourself! If you are the Son of God, come down from the cross." In the same way the chief priests also, along with the scribes and elders, were mocking him, saying, "He saved others; he cannot save himself.... Let him come down from the cross now, and we will believe in him. He trusts in God; let God deliver him now, if he wants to...."

—Matthew 27:32–43a, adapt.

Silence

Leader 1: From noon on, darkness came over the whole land until three in the afternoon. And about three o'clock Jesus cried with a loud voice,

Leader 2: "Eli, Eli, lema sabachthani?"
"My God, my God, why have you forsaken me?"

Leader 1: When some of the bystanders heard it, they said, "This man is calling for Elijah." At once one of them ran and got a sponge, filled it with sour wine, put it on a stick, and gave it to him to drink. But the others said, "Wait, let us see whether Elijah will come to save him." Then Jesus cried again with a loud voice and breathed his last. At that moment the curtain of the temple was torn in two, from top to bottom. The earth shook, and the rocks were split. Now when the centurion and those with him, who were keeping watch over Jesus, saw the earthquake and what took place, they were terrified and said, "Truly this man was a son of God!"

—Matthew 27:45–54

Silence

Leader 1: Lord Jesus, to you we live, to you we suffer, to you we die. Yours will we be in life and in death.

Please depart in silence.

Chapter Six

Way of the Cross

Including:

A Liturgy for Good Friday

A Liturgy for Stations of the Cross

Good Friday observances in diverse traditions take a variety of forms and expressions: procession of the cross, stations of the cross, veneration of the cross, and official Good Friday liturgies that may or may not include any of the former. Sometimes several congregations will join together for denominational or ecumenical Good Friday observances, the traditional three-hour "seven last words" format being the most familiar. Worshipers are invited to come and go for any or all of the seven segments. However, such an approach hardly creates a sense of community within the assembly. Moreover, the collection of "seven last words" comprises lections from all four Gospels, and such a collage does not honor the unique integrity of the Gospels themselves. The liturgy included here proposes one service that includes a procession of the cross, stations to which those who desire may join in the walk, and opportunity for corporate and individual veneration of the cross.

In the religious traditions of some cultures the procession of the cross weaves its way throughout the community. In this liturgy, a rough-hewn cross of about six feet in length, perhaps fabricated by some of the youth of the church, is carried by several people into the church. Since it also will be carried throughout the reading of two chapters of John's Gospel, it may be appropriate for several teams to be assigned to be the carriers. The act of physically carrying the cross is itself a form of prayer. The entrance is accompanied by the ancient hymn for Good Friday, "Pange lingua," by Venantius Fortunatus (530–609). This hymn appears in many translations in hymnals of many traditions, Roman Catholic and Protestant. It appears here as a composite of several translations. The text may

76

be sung to the traditional tune PICARDY, or to a more contemporary one, FORTUNATUS NEW, by Carl Schalk. The "Pange lingua" rescues Good Friday from a morbid introspection on Christ's death by lifting up the metaphor of the tree of life from the first and the last books of the Bible. The cross of death is juxtaposed with the tree of life and thus is transformed from a mere symbol of hatred and death into one of redemption and life.

The two Scripture lections appointed in the *Revised Common Lectionary* for Good Friday in each of the three years in the cycle (Isaiah 52:13–53:12 and Hebrews 10:16–25 or Hebrews 4:14–16) are used here liturgically as part of the penitential rite.

The liturgy of stations of the cross may be unfamiliar to many mainline Protestants. Its origins come from the practice of pilgrims to Jerusalem who paused for prayer at a variety of locations that, tradition said, Jesus had passed by on his way to Golgotha. In some of the traditional liturgies for stations of the cross, the number of stations is fixed at fourteen, and the lections that accompany them have their origins in both canonical Scripture and pious legends. This liturgy, however, is shaped by the Gospel Lesson for Good Friday, which is the same each year in the *Revised Common Lectionary,* namely, John 18:1 through John 19:42. The lection is divided here into eight segments, one designated to be read at each station.

One will note that the word "adapted" appears after each reference. This indicates that the texts have been slightly altered wherever the word "Jews," appears in the New Revised Standard Version text. This alteration attempts to mitigate what often is seen as anti-Semitism in the Gospel of John, implying that the Jews as a race or nation were responsible for Jesus' death. I have kept the Gospel's words "King of the Jews" Pilate's term of derision that eventually became the mocking shout of the crowd.

The assembly's response to each of the eight readings is the traditional Trisagion ("Holy God, Holy and mighty, Holy immortal One, have mercy on us"), which is traced as far back as the middle of the fifth century. It may be spoken or sung in unison to the accompanying melody. The melody may be copied with the text of this liturgy from the CD-ROM for insertion into a worship folder or bulletin. A four-part setting for S-A-T-B, which also may serve as a keyboard accompaniment, may be found on page 172. It also may be sung a cappella, either the melody line alone, or in four-part harmony. It may be sung as is printed or, as in some traditions, three times. Although there is a significant nonverbal communication that occurs during the physical walk from station to station, those who do not desire or cannot physically make the walk nevertheless can participate in the liturgy by remaining in their seats. People should not be forced.

The stations may be identified with simple crosses placed on the wall. Or children may draw pictures of what each of the segments of the Gospel story communicates to them, and these may be mounted on the walls. Or copies of famous artwork appropriate to the texts may be placed at each station. Or with even greater electronic sophistication, projected images may signal each station, but such requires sufficient set-up of the equipment and rehearsal of those who will be the technicians during the liturgy. Or even simply moving to various spots throughout the church will be sufficient. The movement is more important than the identifying symbols and signs.

The stations of the cross rite can be lifted out of the Good Friday liturgy for observances that may occur other than on Good Friday. If such is the case, the service begins with the Penitence rite, eliminates the hymn "Go to Dark Gethsemane," and concludes with the hymn "When I Survey the Wondrous Cross," intercessions, the Lord's Prayer, and a sending rite. The lections from John's Gospel are appropriate for any devotional observance, including a private walk of stations, for they proclaim the message of God's wondrous deed in Christ and draw participants into the meaning of this great mystery by either hearing or reading the texts while walking the way of the cross and allowing the walk to become a means of blessing. Hence, this liturgy does not include a sermon or homily. The eight segments of the Gospel account may be read by eight different readers, or one reader may read all eight segments. The worship folder or bulletin should list only the references to the eight readings. The texts included here and on the accompanying CD-ROM are for the readers and leaders only. The texts can be highlighted and deleted when the worship folders or bulletins are prepared. The intention is that the texts be *heard* in the midst of the corporate assembly and not followed along privately in printed form. No introductions are necessary; the reader simply reads the text. For those who are hearing impaired, or if the liturgy is used for an individual devotional walking of the stations, the texts may be included in separate bulletins.

A corporate liturgy for the veneration of the cross also may seem strange to mainline Protestants. However, I know that many Christians stand or sit before the cross in private devotion and veneration. The focus, obviously, is not on the object itself as some magical fetish, but on what the cross symbolizes: God's sacrificial love given the world through the death and resurrection of Jesus Christ. The veneration that here is prefaced with the suggested singing of Isaac Watts's beloved hymn, "When I Survey the Wondrous Cross," includes the possibility for individuals to go to the cross or to do whatever their individual piety urges them to do. Throughout the history of the church people have found themselves moved by the Spirit to engage in a variety of ways, including tactile ones, of engaging with the cross. This should not be forced, but people should be given the opportunity to express their individual spiritual needs. During this period of private veneration, a choir or soloist may sing or chant the traditional Solemn Reproaches of the Cross, and the assembly may respond to each with the Trisagion, which was sung or said during the reading of the Gospel at the stations. Or a soloist or choir may sing a hymn or anthem such as "Were You There When They Crucified My Lord?" This is not a time for performance, but for musical offerings that lead the whole assembly to prayer. The veneration is not only an expression of individual piety and prayer but also the time for the assembly to pray together and to offer their intercessions for the whole world. The response to each petition, "In your mercy, O God, hear our prayer," may be sung to the tune provided. The keyboard accompaniment may be found on page 178. The response also may be spoken. The veneration, then, is really an act of prayer, individual and corporate, and it concludes with the Lord's Prayer, either said or sung by the assembly.

Since Good Friday services in many communities are ecumenical experiences, the liturgical expressions and hymns in the following liturgy are part of the ecumenical tradition. The ancient hymns included here come from a time before the church was separated, West from East, and before the fragmentations that continue to divide the body of Christ. They become a witness of our unity before the cross of Jesus.

A LITURGY FOR GOOD FRIDAY
CD-ROM 6.1.1

A large rough-hewn cross may be carried into the worship space in prominent view of the assembly. As the cross is carried in, the leader's words may be spoken by those who are carrying the cross or by a presiding liturgist. There may be pauses between each petition.

Leader: Behold the cross on which has hung the salvation of the whole world.

All: Come, let us worship.

Leader: Behold the cross on which has hung the salvation of the whole world.

All: Come, let us worship.

Leader: Behold the cross on which has hung the salvation of the whole world.

All: Come, let us worship.

All may stand and sing: PICARDY or FORTUNATUS NEW

**All: Sing, my tongue, the glorious battle,
as the victim wins the day.
Now the cross becomes the symbol
of, for us, the victor's way.
Tell how Christ, the world's redeemer,
gives himself in shroud to lay.**

**Thirty years of life completed,
now the human form is spent;
Born to fill this sacred moment,
facing death with full intent,
for the sacrifice of ages,
to the cross the Lamb is sent.**

**God in pity saw us fallen,
shamed and sunk in misery,
when we fell on death by tasting
fruit of the forbidden tree:
then another tree was chosen
which the world from death should free.**

Reader: Then the angel showed me the river of the water of life, bright as crystal, flowing from the throne of God and of the Lamb through the middle of the street of the city. On either side of the river is the tree of life with its twelve kinds of fruit, producing its fruit each month; and the leaves of the tree are for the healing of the nations.   — Revelation 22:1–2

**All: Faithful cross, true sign of triumph,
one and only noble tree!**

None in foliage, none in blossom,
none in fruit your equal be!
Sweetest wood and sweetest iron
sweet weight bearing gracefully.

Bend, O noble Tree, your branches;
let your fibers yielding be,
Let the rigid strength be softened
which by nature was to be,
That the limbs of my dear Jesus
May be stretched most tenderly.

Unto God be praise and blessing:
To the Father and the Son,
To the mighty Spirit, glory—
Ever Three and ever One:
Praise and glory in the highest,
while eternal ages run.

Hymn stanzas: Venantius Honorius Fortunatus (520–609),
trans. composite after John Mason Neale (1818–66);
stanza 3 translation © 1995 The Pilgrim Press; used by permission.

Please be seated.

Leader: Let us pray.

All: **Almighty God, unto whom all hearts are open,
all desires known, and from whom no secrets are hid,
cleanse the thoughts of our hearts
by the inspiration of your Holy Spirit,
that we may perfectly love you,
and worthily magnify your name,
through Christ our Lord. Amen.**   *—Book of Common Prayer*

*Isaiah 52:13–53:12 may be read by four readers situated throughout the assembly. Each
shall stand, one immediately after the other, and read without announcement or citation of
the texts:*

Isaiah 52:13–53:3
Isaiah 53:4–6
Isaiah 53:7–9
Isaiah 53:10–12

After the final reading a period of silence shall be observed.

Water may be poured into the font or bowl, and the service continues:

Leader: Lord, have mercy on us.

All: **Christ, have mercy on us.**

Leader: Lord, have mercy on us.

Leader: This is the covenant that I will make with them, says the Lord:
          I will put my laws in their hearts,
          and I will write them on their minds,
          I will remember their sins no more.

An evergreen branch may be dipped into the water in the font and the water sprinkled over those assembled.

Leader: Therefore, my friends,
          since we have confidence to enter the sanctuary by the blood of Jesus,
          by the new and living way that he opened for us,
          and since we have a great priest over the house of God,
          let us approach with a true heart in full assurance of faith,
          with our hearts sprinkled clean from an evil conscience
          and our bodies washed with pure water.
          Let us hold fast to the confession of our hope without wavering,
          for the One who has promised is faithful.
                              —Hebrews 10:16–17, 19–23, adapt.

Or

Leader: Since, then, we have a great high priest
          who has passed through the heavens,
          Jesus, the Son of God, let us hold fast to our confession.
          For we do not have a high priest
          who is unable to sympathize with our weaknesses,
          but we have one who in every respect has been tested as we are,
          yet without sin.
          Let us therefore approach the throne of grace with boldness,
          so that we may receive mercy
          and find grace to help in time of need.   —Hebrews 4:14–16

Silence

Leader: Jesus said, "If any want to become my followers, let them deny themselves
          and take up their cross and follow me."   —Mark 8:34

A LITURGY FOR
STATIONS OF THE CROSS
CD-ROM 6.2.2

Those in the assembly who desire may join a procession as the cross is carried to the first station, and all may sing:

REDHEAD NO. 76

> Go to dark Gethsemane, all who feel the tempter's power;
> your Redeemer's conflict see, watch with him one bitter hour;
> turn not from his griefs away, learn of Jesus Christ to pray.
>
> Follow to the judgment hall, view the Lord of life arraigned,
> O the wormwood and the gall! O the pangs his soul sustained:
> Shun not suffering, shame, or loss; learn of Christ to bear the cross.
>
> Calvary's mournful mountain climb; there, adoring at his feet,
> mark the miracle of time, God's own sacrifice complete;
> "It is finished!" hear him cry; learn from Jesus how to die.

Words: Richard Redhead, 1853, alt.

Gospel Text: John 18:1–11, adapted

Reader: [Jesus] went out with his disciples across the Kidron valley to a place where there was a garden, which he and his disciples entered. Now Judas, who betrayed him, also knew the place, because Jesus often met there with his disciples. So Judas brought a detachment of soldiers together with police from the chief priests and the Pharisees, and they came there with lanterns and torches and weapons. Then Jesus, knowing all that was to happen to him, came forward and asked them, "Whom are you looking for?" They answered, "Jesus of Nazareth." Jesus replied, "I am he." Judas, who betrayed him, was standing with them. When Jesus said to them, "I am he," they stepped back and fell to the ground. Again he asked them, "Whom are you looking for?" And they said, "Jesus of Nazareth." Jesus answered, "I told you that I am he. So if you are looking for me, let these men go." This was to fulfill the word that he had spoken, "I did not lose a single one of those whom you gave me." Then Simon Peter, who had a sword, drew it, struck the high priest's slave, and cut off his right ear. The slave's name was Malchus. Jesus said to Peter, "Put your sword back into its sheath. Am I not to drink the cup that the Father has given me?"

Silence

Leader: We adore you, O Christ, and we bless you.

All: **By your holy cross you have redeemed the world.**

As the cross is carried to another station, those who desire may follow and say or sing:

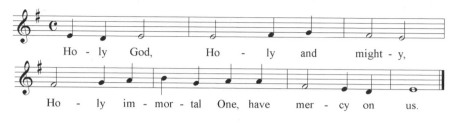

Ho - ly God, Ho - ly and might - y,

Ho - ly im - mor - tal One, have mer - cy on us.

Words: *Trisagion* c. 434 AD; Music: F. Russell Mitman, 2005

Gospel Text: John 18:12–27, adapted

Reader: So the soldiers, their officer, and the Jewish police arrested Jesus and bound him. First they took him to Annas, who was the father-in-law of Caiaphas, the high priest that year. Caiaphas was the one who had advised the Judeans that it was better to have one person die for the people.

Simon Peter and another disciple followed Jesus. Since that disciple was known to the high priest, he went with Jesus into the courtyard of the high priest, but Peter was standing outside at the gate. So the other disciple, who was known to the high priest, went out, spoke to the woman who guarded the gate, and brought Peter in. The woman said to Peter, "You are not also one of this man's disciples, are you?" He said, "I am not." Now the slaves and the police had made a charcoal fire because it was cold, and they were standing around it and warming themselves. Peter also was standing with them and warming himself. Then the high priest questioned Jesus about his disciples and about his teaching. Jesus answered, "I have spoken openly to the world; I have always taught in synagogues and in the temple. . . . I have said nothing in secret. Why do you ask me? Ask those who heard what I said to them; they know what I said." When he had said this, one of the police standing nearby struck Jesus on the face, saying, "Is that how you answer the high priest?" Jesus answered, "If I have spoken wrongly, testify to the wrong. But if I have spoken rightly, why do you strike me?" Then Annas sent him bound to Caiaphas the high priest. Now Simon Peter was standing and warming himself. They asked him, "You are not also one of his disciples, are you?" He denied it and said, "I am not." One of the slaves of the high priest, a relative of the man whose ear Peter had cut off, asked, "Did I not see you in the garden with him?" Again Peter denied it, and at that moment the cock crowed.

Silence

Leader: We adore you, O Christ, and we bless you.

All: **By your holy cross you have redeemed the world.**

As the cross is carried to another station, those who desire may follow and say or sing:

> **Holy God,**
> **Holy and mighty,**
> **Holy immortal One,**
> **have mercy on us.**

Gospel Text: John 18:28–40, adapted

Reader: Then they took Jesus from Caiaphas to Pilate's headquarters. It was early in the morning. They themselves did not enter the headquarters, so as to avoid ritual defilement and to be able to eat the Passover. So Pilate went out to them and said, "What accusation do you bring against this man?" They answered, "If this man were not a criminal, we would not have handed him over to you." Pilate said to them, "Take him yourselves and judge him according to your law." The Jewish officials replied, "We are not permitted to put anyone to death." (This was to fulfill what Jesus had said when he indicated the kind of death he was to die.) Then Pilate entered the headquarters again, summoned Jesus, and asked him, "Are you the King of the Jews?" Jesus answered, "Do you ask this on your own, or did others tell you about me?" Pilate replied, "I am not a Jew, am I? Your own nation and the chief priests have handed you over to me. What have you done?" Jesus answered, "My kingdom is not from this world. If my kingdom were from this world, my followers would be fighting to keep me from being handed over to the Jewish officials. But as it is, my kingdom is not from here." Pilate asked him, "So you are a king?" Jesus answered, "You say that I am a king. For this I was born, and for this I came into the world, to testify to the truth. Everyone who belongs to the truth listens to my voice." Pilate asked him, "What is truth?"

After he had said this, he went out to the Jewish officials again and told them, "I find no case against him. But you have a custom that I release someone for you at the Passover. Do you want me to release for you the King of the Jews?" They shouted in reply, "Not this man, but Barabbas!" Now Barabbas was a bandit.

Silence

Leader: We adore you, O Christ, and we bless you.

All: **By your holy cross you have redeemed the world.**

As the cross is carried to another station, those who desire may follow and say or sing:

> **Holy God,**
> **Holy and mighty,**
> **Holy immortal One,**
> **have mercy on us.**

Gospel Text: John 19:1–11, adapted

Reader: Then Pilate took Jesus and had him flogged. And the soldiers wove a crown of thorns and put it on his head, and they dressed him in a purple robe. They kept coming up to him, saying, "Hail, King of the Jews!" and striking him on the face. Pilate went out again and said to them, "Look, I am bringing him out to you to let you know that I find no case against him." So Jesus came out, wearing the crown of thorns and the purple robe. Pilate said to them, "Here is the man!" When the chief priests and the police saw him, they shouted, "Crucify him! Crucify him!" Pilate said to them, "Take him yourselves and crucify him; I find no case against him." The Jewish officials answered him, "We have a law, and according to that law he ought to die because he has claimed to be the Son of God." Now when Pilate heard this, he was more afraid than ever. He entered his headquarters again and asked Jesus, "Where are you from?" But Jesus gave him no answer. Pilate therefore said to him, "Do you refuse to speak to me? Do you not know that I have power to release you, and power to crucify you?" Jesus answered him, "You would have no power over me unless it had been given you from above; therefore the one who handed me over to you is guilty of a greater sin."

Silence

Leader: We adore you, O Christ, and we bless you.

All: **By your holy cross you have redeemed the world.**

As the cross is carried to another station, those who desire may follow and say or sing:

> **Holy God,**
> **Holy and mighty,**
> **Holy immortal One,**
> **have mercy on us.**

Gospel Text: John 19:12–16a, adapted

Reader: From then on Pilate tried to release him, but the Jewish officials cried out, "If you release this man, you are no friend of the emperor. Everyone who claims to be a king sets himself against the emperor."

    When Pilate heard these words, he brought Jesus outside and sat on the judge's bench at a place called The Stone Pavement, or in Hebrew Gabbatha. Now it was the day of Preparation for the Passover; and it was about noon. He said to the crowd, "Here is your King!" They cried out, "Away with him! Away with him! Crucify him!" Pilate asked them, "Shall I crucify your King?" The chief priests answered, "We have no king but the emperor." Then he handed him over to them to be crucified.

Silence

Leader: We adore you, O Christ, and we bless you.

All: **By your holy cross you have redeemed the world.**

As the cross is carried to another station, those who desire may follow and say or sing:

> **Holy God,**
> **Holy and mighty,**
> **Holy immortal One,**
> **have mercy on us.**

Gospel Text: John 19:16b–27, adapted

Reader: So they took Jesus; and carrying the cross by himself, he went out to what is called The Place of the Skull, which in Hebrew is called Golgotha. There they crucified him, and with him two others, one on either side, with Jesus between them. Pilate also had an inscription written and put on the cross. It read, "Jesus of Nazareth, the King of the Jews." Many of the people of Jerusalem read this inscription, because the place where Jesus was crucified was near the city; and it was written in Hebrew, in Latin, and in Greek. Then the chief priests said to Pilate, "Do not write, 'The King of the Jews,' but, 'This man said, I am King of the Jews.'" Pilate answered, "What I have written I have written." When the soldiers had crucified Jesus, they took his clothes and divided them into four parts, one for each soldier. They also took his tunic; now the tunic was seamless, woven in one piece from the top. So they said to one another, "Let us not tear it, but cast lots for it to see who will get it." This was to fulfill what the scripture says, "They divided my clothes among themselves, and for my clothing they cast lots." And that is what the soldiers did. Meanwhile, standing near the cross of Jesus were his mother, and his mother's sister, Mary the wife of Clopas, and Mary Magdalene. When Jesus saw his mother and the disciple whom he loved standing beside her, he said to his mother, "Woman, here is your son." Then he said to the disciple, "Here is your mother." And from that hour the disciple took her into his own home.

Silence

Leader: We adore you, O Christ, and we bless you.

All: **By your holy cross you have redeemed the world.**

As the cross is carried to another station, those who desire may follow and say or sing:

> **Holy God,**
> **Holy and mighty,**
> **Holy immortal One,**
> **have mercy on us.**

Gospel Text: John 19:28–37, adapted

Reader: After this, when Jesus knew that all was now finished, he said (in order to fulfill the scripture), "I am thirsty." A jar full of sour wine was standing there. So they put a sponge full of the wine on a branch of hyssop and held it to his mouth. When Jesus had received the wine, he said, "It is finished." Then he bowed his head and gave up his spirit.

    Since it was the day of Preparation, the Jewish officials did not want the bodies left on the cross during the sabbath, especially because that sabbath was a day of great solemnity. So they asked Pilate to have the legs of the crucified men broken and the bodies removed. Then the soldiers came and broke the legs of the first and of the other who had been crucified with him. But when they came to Jesus and saw that he was already dead, they did not break his legs. Instead, one of the soldiers pierced his side with a spear, and at once blood and water came out. (He who saw this has testified so that you also may believe. His testimony is true, and he knows that he tells the truth.) These things occurred so that the scripture might be fulfilled, "None of his bones shall be broken." And again another passage of scripture says, "They will look on the one whom they have pierced."

Silence

Leader: We adore you, O Christ, and we bless you.

All: **By your holy cross you have redeemed the world.**

As the cross is carried to another station, those who desire may follow and say or sing:

> **Holy God,**
> **Holy and mighty,**
> **Holy immortal One,**
> **have mercy on us.**

Gospel Text: John 19:38–42, adapted

Reader: After these things, Joseph of Arimathea, who was a disciple of Jesus, though a secret one because of his fear of the Jewish officials, asked Pilate to let him take away the body of Jesus. Pilate gave him permission; so he came and removed his body. Nicodemus, who had at first come to Jesus by night, also came, bringing a mixture of myrrh and aloes, weighing about a hundred pounds. They took the body of Jesus and wrapped it with the spices in linen cloths, according to the Jewish burial custom. Now there was a garden in the place where he was crucified, and in the garden there was a new tomb in which no one had ever been laid. And so, because it was the Jewish day of Preparation, and the tomb was nearby, they laid Jesus there.

Leader: We adore you, O Christ, and we bless you.

All: By your holy cross you have redeemed the world.

As the cross is carried to a place of veneration before the assembly, those who were part of the procession may be seated, as all sing:

When I survey the wondrous cross   ROCKINGHAM **or** HAMBURG
on which the Prince of Glory died,
My riches gain I count but loss,
and pour contempt on all my pride.

Forbid it, Lord, that I should boast,
save in the death of Christ, my God;
All the vain things that charm me most,
I sacrifice them to his blood.

See! from his head, his hands, his feet,
sorrow and love flow mingled down;
Did e'er such love and sorrow meet,
or thorns compose so rich a crown?

Were the whole realm of nature mine,
that were an offering far too small;
Love so amazing, so divine,
demands my soul, my life, my all.

Words: Isaac Watts, 1707

Time is given for individual venerations. Persons are invited to stand before the cross, to kneel before it, to touch it, to embrace it, or even to kiss it. Some simply may wish to sit in their seats and meditate on it. The Solemn Reproaches may be sung or chanted, and the assembly may respond with the Trisagion, which was sung during the processions to the stations of the cross. The service continues, and the assembly may sit or kneel for the intercessions:

Leader: The Lord be with you.

All: And also with you.

Leader: Let us pray.

Leader: Holy God, who assured us in Christ Jesus
                that whatever we ask in his name will be granted to us
                and who promised to intercede for us through the Holy Spirit,
                hear now the prayers of your people.

Silence

Leader: For the world you have fashioned
and every living thing formed by your creating hand,
that all your creatures may be in harmony.

Response:

singing or speaking

In your mer - cy, O God, hear our prayer.

Silence

Leader: For the peoples of earth,
that they may acknowledge the common humanity that unites them
and learn the ways of peace,

Response:

singing or speaking
In your mercy, O God, hear our prayer.

Silence

Leader: For the leaders of all nations and states and communities,
and especially for _____ ,
that they may be led to govern wisely
and to hasten the day when justice and righteousness shall fill all the earth,

Response:

singing or speaking
In your mercy, O God, hear our prayer.

Silence

Leader: For one holy catholic church throughout the whole wide earth, and
especially for _____ (*partner churches in foreign lands,
missionaries, denominational officials, ecclesiastical meetings, local church
pastors and people may be mentioned*), that the body of Christ may be built
up in love, and faith nourished through Word and Sacrament,

Response:

singing or speaking
In your mercy, O God, hear our prayer.

Silence

Leader: For those who find themselves victims of forces beyond their control:
for those oppressed in mind or body,
for those crushed by life's sudden changes,
for those enslaved by controlling ideologies or chemical addictions,
that they may be assured of your power to save and to free,

Response:

> *singing or speaking*
> **In your mercy, O God, hear our prayer.**

Silence

Leader: For those who suffer from the ravages of illness in body or mind,
           for those who anxiously await diagnoses,
           for those confined by infirmity, and especially for _____,
           that they may be comforted by your abiding presence amid their pain
           and find wholeness by your healing hand laid upon them,

Response:

> *singing or speaking*
> **In your mercy, O God, hear our prayer.**

Silence

Leader: For those who are dying,
           for those to whom death has caused a great emptiness,
           and especially for _____,
           that they may be touched by a resurrecting peace
           that now passes understanding,

Response:

> *singing or speaking*
> **In your mercy, O God, hear our prayer.**

Silence

Leader: For ourselves and the things that,
           deeply hidden within the recesses of our minds,
           we now pour out before you in silence:

Silence

Response:

> *singing or speaking*

In your   mer - cy, O   God,   hear our   prayer, and   grant   us your peace.   A - men.

Music copyright © 1987 F. Russell Mitman

Leader: God so loved the world that he gave his only Son, that everyone who
           believes in him may not perish but have eternal life. Indeed, God did not
           send the Son into the world to condemn the world, but in order that the
           world might be saved through him.   —John 3:16–17

All may rise to sing:

WONDROUS LOVE

What wondrous love is this, O my soul! O my soul!
What wondrous love is this, O my soul!
What wondrous love is this! that Christ should come in bliss
      to bear the heavy cross for my soul, for my soul,
      to bear the heavy cross for my soul!

To God and to the Lamb I will sing, I will sing,
to God and to the Lamb I will sing, I will sing,
to God and to the Lamb who is the great I Am,
      while millions join the theme, I will sing, I will sing;
      while millions join the theme, I will sing.

And when from death I'm free, I'll sing on, I'll sing on,
and when from death I'm free, I'll sing on, I'll sing on!
And when from death I'm free, I'll sing and joyful be,
      and through eternity I'll sing on, I'll sing on,
      and through eternity I'll sing on!

Words: 19th-century American, alt. First published in Mercer's Cluster, 1836

Or

HERZLIEBSTER JESU

Ah, holy Jesus, how have you offended,
      that mortal judgment has on you descended?
By foes derided, by your own rejected,
      O most afflicted!

Who was the guilty? Who brought this upon you?
      It is my treason, Jesus, that has slain you.
And I, dear Jesus, I it was denied you;
      I crucified you.

For me, kind Jesus, was your incarnation,
      your mortal sorrow, and your life's oblation,
Your death of anguish and your bitter passion,
      for my salvation.

Therefore, kind Jesus, since I cannot pay you,
      I do adore you, and will ever praise you,
Think on your pity and your love unswerving,
      not my deserving.

Words: Johann Heermann, 1630, para. Robert Bridges, 1899, alt.

All depart in silence.

Chapter Seven

Marriage

Including:

*A Liturgy for the Celebration of Marriage
Including Options for a Marriage Renewal Service*

A Liturgy for Eucharist in a Marriage Service

Of all worship acts, perhaps none is more in need of rigorous thought and liturgical updating than the celebration of marriage. The worship commissions of some denominations have attempted liturgical renewal, while others have tried to reword their old forms. Many ministers, frustrated with the inadequacies of the liturgical inheritance, have devised wedding ceremonies of their own. Couples have pasted together collages of marital expressions from sources both sacred and secular. Some clergy have demanded couples to adhere to orders that no longer express the couples' concept of what a wedding ought to be. In revolt, many couples have sought out those who will accept their ideas. The general cultural perception of marriage, gilded by Hollywood and the media, has provided fertile ground for entrepreneurs to market all sorts of wedding paraphernalia. Organists and church musicians have been mortified by the music sometimes requested, and they either refuse to accommodate or cringe quietly under the organ bench. Parents, especially mothers of the brides-to-be, have definite ideas of what a wedding should be, or should have been, and have created tensions in which ministers have been forced to arbitrate, usually to the satisfaction of none. In this state of general chaos, the most acceptable solution has been to resort to doing it the way it has always been done, and hence no service of the church has been left so basically unchanged, despite all the energies expended to do something different.

I presume part of the confusion is the result of two, sometimes conflicting, aspects of marriage, which, especially on the American scene,

93

have been welded together. On the one hand there is the societal need to *legalize* marriage, and on the other hand there is the need of the religious community to *bless* marriage. In some parts of the world these two different needs are met by separate exercises, one in a magisterial setting and the other in an ecclesiastical one. The first is required of everyone; the second is optional for those of a religious bent. However, despite all our words about separation of church and state, in America generally both exercises occur simultaneously. The minister is officiant not only in his or her churchly office but also as a deputy of the state. And since contemporary culture deems a civil marriage by the local magistrate as something not quite proper, in many cases the need to legalize marriage forces people into a faith conception that may be quite at odds with their cultural perception of a wedding. Hence, those who consider religious expressions irrelevant superimpose the cultural symbols they find meaningful onto something that has a quite different intent and integrity. I see no immediate solution to the problem. We will have to accept the two forces and try to provide viable forms for those in the religious community who desire their marriage to occur in faith forms, and we will have to work up alternative cultural forms for those who see marriage primarily as a cultic and civil rite. Since the perspective of this book is corporate worship, the model order for celebrating marriage presented in this chapter is an attempt at the former. I shall leave it to others more versed in civil religion to provide the latter.

The issue has become more clouded in recent years by the cultural rhetoric around what different and competing ideologies perceive the meaning of the word "marriage" to be. Attempts to legalize same-sex unions and to identify them as "marriage" have polarized society in the United States and have initiated efforts to codify "marriage" in state and federal laws and constitutions. I do not wish to enter into the political, and sometimes ecclesiastical, debates around the so-called "same-sex marriage" issue. Those who wish to adapt the liturgical materials here for use in same-sex union rites may feel free to do so. The presupposition on which these liturgical expressions are shaped is that "marriage" is the liturgical action of the Christian community uniting two people in a sacred covenant and asking God to bless their relationship with each other and with the whole community.

I hope that what I have just said does not obscure the reality that marriage, even when celebrated in faith forms, does have about it a legalization perspective. The terms "take," "covenant," "promise," and "witness," and their nonverbal symbols are legal remnants of a former world that knew no distinction between church and state. In ancient Israel, and almost throughout all Christian history, society's needs for legalization were rooted and grounded in a holistic view of reality that was conceptually religious. Today, given the American phenomenon of vesting magisterial rights with the minister, marriage in the community of faith still has, by necessity, a legalizing perspective. However, it seems to me that our approach to the liturgical actions celebrating marriage must originate from a *theological* model, and whatever civil legalizations that are necessary within those liturgical actions need to be accomplished under laws of the state. In my mind, if the necessary legalization were handled by civil authorities, the church community would be freed up to be about its rightful responsibility to celebrate a sacred rite of blessing a relationship initiated and sealed by God.

Marriage in the Judeo-Christian tradition is built upon faith's understanding of the role and purpose of the family. Genesis tells us that Abraham, because of the divine intervention that made him partner with God in the everlasting covenant, is promised a son through whom and by whose progeny the covenant will be perpetuated. The uniqueness of the birth is accentuated by the symbolic change of his wife's name. By divine decree, Sarah is to be "mother of nations." Along with "Father" Abraham, she is to give birth to a family line that will become the future context for the continuation of the divine-human interaction. In the New Testament, Matthew and Luke clearly identify the divine-human at-one-ness in the context of a family and the human relationships that result from childbirth and parenting. Even though the church has tended to shortchange the role of Joseph, the family tree guaranteeing Jesus' authenticity as Messiah is traced by Matthew via Joseph, back through David, to the "father" of the extended family, Abraham. Again, the family is both the result and the context of the divine-human interaction. Even Paul (if he indeed authored the Letter to the Ephesians) goes so far as to use the husband-wife relationship as a paradigm for the relationship between Christ and his church. The whole biblical witness to what God does with the people of God is couched in family-type language and concepts.

What all this means, to me at least, is that we need to look at marriage primarily in family typologies rather than in romantic or legal conceptions. Liturgically, this means that the structure of the marriage celebration will be quite different from that derived from Hollywood or the courtroom. I have the notion that many traditional Protestant marriage services are really courtroom settings: the couple standing before the "judge" dressed in judicial gown; the "witnesses" standing beside the couple; the family relegated to silence in the gallery; the judge admonishing the couple regarding the terms of the contract and deciding judicially that there is no "just cause why they may not lawfully be joined together." And the whole action takes place solely between the judge and the couple. Superimposed on this scenario are a jumble of Hollywood trappings and scenery to mitigate the harshness of the courtroom atmosphere. I would even be so brash as to infer that perhaps one of the reasons so many marriages end up in the courtroom is that they begin there in the first place!

The structure of a marriage service based on a family typology, however, will be quite different. It will begin with the families gathering to worship God and to celebrate the marriage of two of their number in the context of worship. There is ample justification for the liturgy for marriage to take place during a regular Sunday service. The liturgy in this chapter is designed to be used in a Sunday service if desired, although the weight of tradition will militate strongly against such use in the foreseeable future. In most instances the marriage service will be a separate one, and there is no reason why it should not be a valid service in its own right.

The model order included here begins not with a judicial statement but with the family of faith praising and praying and telling the story of its faith. The order is the classic *ordo* of Christian worship that is part of any worship event. The singing of an entrance hymn is quite appropriate, although there needs to be a sufficient number of people present for good singing. Members of the family may read the lessons, and the minister may deliver a brief homily. In this model order, the reading of Scripture and the homily replace the traditional "dearly beloved" injunctions about marriage. It seems far more appropriate to allow the Scriptures to address the marriage family and to say what needs to be said in a pastoral and even personal way than to be satisfied with some "canned" exhortation that has about it a judicial air and that nobody tends to listen to anyway.

If marriage is, in a total sense, a family affair, the whole family present are not spectators to but participants in the liturgy. Bulletins, at least in my neck of the woods, are now more the norm than the exception for weddings, and everyone present can participate in the service. Since the congregation at most weddings — at least at those I have been a part of — is made up of the extended family of the couple, it is quite appropriate for them to pray in unison the prayer of the blessing and the Lord's Prayer. The family prays for God's blessing and is blessed. It is appropriate also for them to welcome the couple and to pledge them their support, to pray for the renewal of all other relationships in the family, and to exchange greetings of peace — even the sign of the kiss which need not be restricted to the marriage couple!

Out of a pastoral concern I have attempted to be as inclusive as possible in the model that follows. On the occasions when there are children from a previous marriage or marriages, I feel they ought to be recognized and included in the new relationship being established. Likewise, parents should not be relegated to the front pew, worse yet, set fenced apart by the center aisle. Parents must be recognized and allowed to give their blessing to the marriage. They have a lot more at stake in this new relationship than symbolized in the father-of-the-bride's consent. Furthermore, "giving away the bride" is an archaic custom that negates the role of parents and harkens back to the days when men "gave away" their daughters as chattel.

The reader will note that the order is designed to be used not only for the service of marriage per se but also as a service of marriage renewal. Sometimes couples need a way to celebrate reconciliation or to bless a civil marriage. Sadly, most denominational liturgies completely ignore these pastoral acts. There are also occasions (perhaps as often as yearly) when the family wants to celebrate a marriage anniversary and even when the whole congregation engages in a liturgical expression of renewal of marriage vows and family commitments. These pastoral dimensions have shaped the common order that follows. It may be used, with the appropriate alternatives and deletions, for these acts as well as for the normative marriage service.

The reader will detect a similarity between this order and the one for baptism in chapter 1, and this is not mere coincidence. Both are acts in which the self-giving God establishes new relationships. In baptism God signs and seals us into the covenant of grace and initiates us into the body of Christ. In marriage God also acts to establish a new relationship between two people *within* the community of the baptized. In baptism we are initiated into the family of God, and in marriage God acts to continue the family. I don't want to become embroiled here in the age-old argument about sacraments versus rites. To those who want to preserve the traditional distinction, I suggest that marriage can be viewed as an extension of the baptismal covenant — a new family is established within the wider context of the whole family of the covenant. Yet even in this view marriage cannot be relegated to a mere ceremony that we mortals perform. On the other hand, those who desire to view marriage from a sacramental perspective need to see it not as an entity in itself but as interrelated with baptism. The establishing of a new relationship (family) between two people in marriage presupposes the extended family into which the two were initiated by baptism. From either perspective the significance of the action is preserved. God acts in marriage to bring a new relationship into being, a relationship that cannot exist in its totality without God's doing.

Also, like baptism, marriage is a one-time act that has about it an unconditional nature. Marriage is not a human experiment; it is not an interim arrangement as long as romance jiggles the heart; it is not a legal agreement to get through an income tax loophole. One wonders what would be the societal consequences if marriage were held as something that God effects. Perhaps the family of faith would not be so ready to let two persons walk away from each other. Perhaps the family of faith would be more eager to suffer through conflict to some resolution, and if it be divorce, to share in the pain of that final aborting of the relationship; if it be reunion, to celebrate reconciliation and reuniting. There are religious communities where the whole family supports the two of its number in conflict, and statistically their track record is far superior than that of those of us who don't want to interfere. How un-family-like it is for us to leave it up to the couple to fend for themselves. The sin in such a situation is not one of commission by the couple as much as it is a sin of omission by the faith family. Thus, it is the faith family that needs repentance and forgiveness. Maybe this situation also reflects a basic misunderstanding of and lack of appreciation for the action of baptism in which the whole family of faith is washed and made new. It is for these reasons, then, that opportunities for renewal of baptism and renewal of marriage ought to be part of our common liturgical practice.

In addition to the sacramental nature of marriage, there is also the contractual perspective on the human side. God makes two people one in marriage, but two people need to make some kind of human contract with each other that verbalizes and dramatizes their intent. Likewise, the whole family needs some tangible indication that these two, and these two alone, are the rightful marriage partners. Both needs are satisfied by the vows. Vows are mutual promises to be and to do certain things. Each partner pledges a monogamous relationship and promises a faithfulness that is more than a temporal arrangement. Yes, the vows promise love, but they make that love concrete. The vows, that is, the words of the marriage agreement or covenant, are not sacrosanct in themselves; thus, it is quite appropriate for those who so desire to state in their own words their contract with each other, as long as there is some acknowledgment of the inviolability of that promise. The vows are accompanied by the joining of right hands, a nonverbal act (it also guarantees that the couple will look at each other and not at the minister) that may be reinforced with the giving and receiving of rings. Together with the giving of the rings, the joining of right hands is the human ratification of the marital agreement. The officiant does not "marry" the couple; they marry each other by mutually consenting to the agreement. The role of the minister is merely to announce publicly and, in the magisterial role, legally, that the contract has been effected. The order in this chapter also includes promises by the whole family to support two of their number in a new and fragile relationship. The family promises are a liturgical attempt to recognize the crucial role of the extended family.

Sometimes couples express the desire to receive holy communion as part of the marriage act. Given the sacramental nature of marriage and the tradition of liturgical practice in certain churches, the celebration of the Eucharist is a natural and fitting part of marriage. However, if there is to be a celebration of the Eucharist, which by its very definition is a communal act, the invitation to receive the Communion should be extended to all in the congregation who desire it. The Eucharist is the meal of the whole family and should not be denied to anyone who wants to share in it. When the Eucharist is to be included, following the prayer of marriage renewal, the minister may continue with a Eucharistic prayer. The Lord's Prayer (said or sung by the whole congregation and not just by a soloist) can be delayed until immediately preceding the distribution of the elements. An order for the Eucharist in the marriage service can be found on page 106.

One final word needs to be said regarding the setting of the marriage celebration: it ought to be uncomplicated. So much of the ceremonial trappings that tradition and commercialism have piled on the marriage celebration serve to distract the couple and the congregation from what both are really about. Maybe, as I said earlier, those trappings arose to fill the void of the courtroom setting. White aisle runners once protected gowns from dirty stone floors, but in most churches where the sexton has dutifully vacuumed the rug prior to the service, they are totally unnecessary. Stilted wedding marches make the day appear more like an occult funeral rite than a joyous celebration. Making sure everybody is standing in the proper place at the proper time sometimes consumes more time and energy than pre-marital pastoral care. The setting ought not to be forced. If there are only a dozen or two of the family present, they may stand with the couple or even enter the room with them. The tradition of having the men, including the groom, appear from some side door and stand in a line-up waiting for the women to come down the aisle is more than awkward. Instead, the groom may escort his mother or both parents and sit with them until the bride, if escorted in the procession, reaches the place where he rises and receives her hand from the one escorting her. The attendants, generally paired as couples at the conclusion of the service, also may process as couples at the beginning of the service and either stand together as couples or separate when they have reached the area in which the service will begin. The couple — and attendants — may stand in such a place as to face the congregation rather than the officiant. If the font is located centrally, it may be appropriate for the vows and blessings to take place around it. That's where we were brought into the family — what better place to begin a new family relationship?

The couple and attendants do not necessarily need to stand throughout the service. In many churches, the content of the marriage service has been determined by the length of standing time. Luckily, this is a practice easily corrected. The couple and attendants can be seated prior to the vows and during the Eucharist if it is celebrated. Even portable seating can be used if fixed pews do not lend themselves (as is often the case) to the liturgical action. Members of the wedding party or family may serve as lectors for the lessons and prayers. Movement can take place if there are no architectural barriers. It has always been distressing to me that building committees give so much thought to ensure a long enough aisle for weddings and a proper place for the bride to dress, and yet so little thought to the real action that takes place in the wedding service. In short, the setting ought to be arranged in as uncomplicated a way as possible and ought to facilitate the liturgical action so that both couple and congregation will be about the intention of the day — the joyous celebration of marriage.

A LITURGY FOR THE CELEBRATION OF MARRIAGE INCLUDING OPTIONS FOR A MARRIAGE RENEWAL SERVICE
CD-ROM 7.1.1

If the marriage rite occurs during a service of Word and Sacrament, the couple and their attendants may gather at the font or before the congregation following the sermon and creed/statement of faith. The congregation may sing a hymn during such gathering, and the order for the marriage rite begins with the minister's question of intention to the couple.

If the marriage rite occurs as a separate service, the order is as follows.

Minister: This is the day that the Lord has made!

All: **Let us rejoice and be glad in it!**   — Psalm 118:24

A hymn may be sung by the congregation, or there may be instrumental music. The couple and their party may process. The congregation may stand.

Minister: In the name of the triune God we gather.
             Together, let us pray.

All: **God our creator, by whom every family**
             in heaven and on earth is named,
             with joy we celebrate this day
             and remember your boundless love for your children.
             We praise you for the ties that bind us in your everlasting covenant
             and for the human bonds that unite us with one another.
             When we become careless of precious relationships
             and callous of human needs,
             we pray that we may be forgiven and restored.
             When we enter into new relationships and establish new trusts,
             we ask you to sign and seal them with your loving hand.
             Open our hearts and minds
             to behold the wondrous promises of your grace,
             and assure us of your blessing on your family. Amen.

The congregation may be seated.

Readings from the Scriptures are read. Suggested lections are:

Old Testament
             Genesis 1:26–31
             Genesis 2:15–24
             Song of Solomon 2:10–13, 8:6–7
             Jeremiah 31:31–34

Psalms

> *These may be sung or said responsively between the readings*
> Psalm 8
> Psalm 67
> Psalm 117
> Psalm 128

Epistles

> Romans 12:1–2, 9–18
> 1 Corinthians 13 or 1 Corinthians 13:4–8a
> Ephesians 3:14–19
> 1 John 4:7–12

Gospels

> Matthew 5:1–10
> Mark 10:6–9
> John 2:1–11 (especially if the Eucharist is to be celebrated)
> John 15:1–11 or John 15:1–17

The minister offers a homily based on the lections chosen. The assembly may respond with a creed, a statement of faith, or a covenant. A hymn may be sung. If the marriage occurs during a service of Word and Sacrament, the order begins with the following.

Minister: *addressing the couple*
(*Names*) _____ and _____,
you are two unique persons who have come from separate lives
to be made one by God
and to covenant with each other in a new and lasting relationship.
Are you ready to be married?

Couple: **We are.**

The parents may rise, and the minister may address them:

Minister: (*Names*) _____,
you have given *birth to/parented*
(*Name*) _____ and (*Name*) _____.
You have laughed and cried with them,
disciplined and encouraged them.
They are now ready
option: to leave father and mother and
to be joined to each other.
Do you bless their union,
and do you accept each one's partner
as your very own *son/daughter*?

Parents: **We do.**

Parents may be seated.

If this order is used for the blessing of a civil marriage or for the act of marriage renewal, the minister addresses the couple in the following words:

Minister: (*Names*) _____ and _____ ,
you have come to celebrate God's blessing on your marriage
and to renew the vows you once made with each other.
Are you ready to reaffirm your mutual pledge
and to ask God's continual help in your pilgrimage together?

Couple: We are.

If there are any children by previous marriage(s), the minister may address them.

Minister: (*Name[s]*) _____ ,
we are here to celebrate a new marriage,
and we rejoice that you are part of this new family.
We pray God to give you the love and understanding
to receive *this/these new person(s)* into your own *life/lives.*

The minister then addresses the couple:

Minister: (*Names*) _____ and _____ ,
God has called you together.
Please join your hands,
and before these people make your covenant with each other.

The couple exchanges vows either of their own crafting or according to one of the following. They may speak their vows to each other with or without prompting by the minister.

Each: _____ , in love that has no limit to its endurance,
no end to its trust, no fading of its hope, and that outlasts everything else,
I promise with God's help to be your faithful *husband/wife,*
and I take you to be my *wife/husband.*

Or

Each: _____ , I promise with God's help
to be your faithful *husband/wife:*
to grow with you in a love that has no limit to its endurance,
no end to its trust, no fading of its hope, and that outlasts everything else.

Or

Each: I take you, (*Name*) _____ ,
to be my *wife/husband,* and I promise with God's help
to love and sustain you as long as we both shall live.

Or

Each: (*Name*) _____ , I promise with God's help
          to be your faithful *husband/wife*, from this moment on,
          in sickness and in health, in plenty and in want,
          in joy and in sorrow, until we are parted by death.

Or

Each: (*Name*) _____ , I promise with God's help
          to be your faithful partner in marriage:
          to laugh and to cry with you,
          to rejoice and to hurt with you,
          and to share with you my whole being
          throughout our pilgrimage together.

Or if it is the occasion of marriage renewal or the blessing of a civil marriage:

Each: (*Name*) _____ , with the help of God
          I renew this day my promise to remain for all our days
          your faithful *husband/wife/partner* in marriage.

If a ring or rings are given, the minister may ask:

Minister: What will you give as a sign of your promise?

The minister may add the following prayer.

Minister: May *this ring/these rings,* O God, by your blessing,
           be to the one(s) to whom they are given,
           perpetual symbol(s) of your abiding love
           and of the covenant made this day,
           through Jesus Christ our Lord. Amen.

A ring or rings may be given accompanied by the following words:

Each: (*Name*) _____ ,
          This ring is a sign of my promise.
          I give it to you with my love.

The couple may join right hands, and the minister may lay his or her hands on them.

Minister: (*Names*) _____ and _____ ,
           by the promises you have made in the presence of God and these people,
           you are husband and wife, according to the witness of Christ's church;
           optional: and the laws of this state.
           Love one another as Christ has loved you!

Minister: *addressing the assembly*
           Will you who are witnesses to these promises
           seek by word and deed to nourish
           (*Names*) _____ and _____
           in their life together?

All: **We will.**
    What God has joined together, let no one separate.

                   —Matthew 19:6

Minister: Praise the Lord!

All: **The Lord be praised!**

    The couple may kneel for the blessing.

Minister: Let us pray.

All: **Eternal God, without whose grace no promise is sure:**
    Shower upon (*Names***) _____ and _____**
    the blessings of your Holy Spirit.
    Strengthen them in a faith that never withers.
    Sustain them in a hope that never despairs.
    Support them in a love that never ends.
    And grant that in every promise both they and we
    may remain constant and faithful,
    and live in harmony with all people,
    having the same mind which was in Christ Jesus,
    who came not to be served,
    but to serve and give his life for others. Amen.

Depending on the circumstances and the wishes of the couple, the minister may pray:

Minister: O God, whose Son was laid by loving parents in Bethlehem's manger,
    we ask, if it is your will, to give to
    (*Names*) _____ and _____
    the precious gift of children,
    granting them patience to care for their needs
    and willingness to grow with them in faith, hope, and love.

All: **Amen.**

If there are children of previous marriages, the minister may pray:

Minister: God of all families, we pray for this new family united by marriage.
    Grant them the courage to discover new relationships of trust
    to dispel past hurts and replace past losses,
    and enable them to grow together in new understandings of
    faith, hope, and love.

All: **Amen.**

On all occasions, the minister continues:

Minister: O God, whose Son, Jesus, was a guest at the marriage in Cana of Galilee,
    grant your blessing to all married persons gathered here today,
    that they may find their marriages strengthened by Christ's presence
    and their love renewed by his love.

All: **Amen.**

Minister: Renew also the common bonds that unite your whole family
of all ages, tongues, and races, that we,
being rooted and grounded in love,
may discover more and more
the breadth and length and height and depth of Christ's love
and be filled with all the fullness of your grace.

All: **Amen.**

◆ ◆ ◆

If the Eucharist is celebrated, the service continues with the following.

A LITURGY FOR EUCHARIST
IN A MARRIAGE SERVICE
CD-ROM 7.2.1

The couple(s) may present the bread and wine during the singing of the hymn.

All: *singing, those who are able standing,* NUN DANKET

> **Now thank we all our God with heart and hands and voices,**
> **who wondrous things has done, in whom this world rejoices,**
> **who from our parents' arms, has blessed us on our way**
> **with countless gifts of love, and still is ours today.**
>
> **O may this bounteous God through all our life be near us,**
> **with ever joyful hearts and blessed peace to cheer us,**
> **and keep us in God's grace, and guide us when perplexed,**
> **and free us from all ills in this world and the next.**

Words: Martin Rinckart, 1647, trans. Catherine Winkworth, alt.

Minister: Let the heavens be glad, and let the earth rejoice!

All: **O give thanks to the Lord, who is good;**
God's steadfast love endures for ever! — 1 Chronicles 16:31, 34, adapt.

Minister: We give thanks, O God,
that from the beginning you have created us for life together
and have blessed human relationships with your abundant grace;
through your beloved Son
you have showed us the way to love and to be loved.

We praise you that the same Christ who honored those
at the wedding in Cana of Galilee with a holy presence
is ever present now to bless all who pledge their lives
in love and faithfulness to each other.

We ask you that as the guests at Cana's marriage feast
tasted the water turned into wine,
so also may the presence of your Holy Spirit at this table
transform us and the bread and wine we here offer you,
that in this sacrament we may be at one with the Christ
who fills us with joy and nourishes us in love.

Minister: Blessed be God from everlasting to everlasting!

All: Amen!

And/Or

All: *singing*   NUN DANKET

**All praise and thanks to God who reigns in highest heaven,
to Father and to Son and Spirit now be given,
The one eternal God whom heaven and earth adore,
the God who was, and is, and shall be evermore.**

Words: Martin Rinckart, 1647, trans. Catherine Winkworth, alt.

The congregation may be seated.

The minister recites the words of institution while breaking the bread and pouring the cup.

Minister: As Jesus taught his disciples to pray, we pray together:

**All: Our Father in heaven:
            Hallowed be your name,
            Your kingdom come,
            Your will be done, on earth as in heaven.
            Give us today our daily bread.
            Forgive us our sins, as we forgive those who sin against us.
            Save us from the time of trial, and deliver us from evil.
            For the kingdom, the power, and the glory are yours,
            now and forever. Amen.**

Minister: O taste and see that the Lord is good!
            and/or Come, all things are ready!

*The minister may direct the families and invite those who desire to share in the Communion
to join the wedding party.*

Minister: *administering to the couple first,*
            (*Names*) _____ and _____ ,
            may the living bread of heaven broken for you
            nourish you unto everlasting life.

            (*Names*) _____ and _____ ,
            may the royal wine of heaven poured out for you
            sustain you unto everlasting life.

After all have communed, the minister continues.

Minister: Blessed be the Lord, our God, who does wondrous things!

All: **Blessed be God's glorious name forever;**
may God's glory fill the whole earth! Amen.

—Psalm 72:18–19, adapt.

◆ ◆ ◆

When the Eucharist is not celebrated, the service continues:

Minister: As Jesus taught his disciples to pray, we pray together:

All: **Our Father in heaven:**
Hallowed be your name,
Your kingdom come,
Your will be done, on earth as in heaven.
Give us today our daily bread.
Forgive us our sins, as we forgive those who sin against us.
Save us from the time of trial, and deliver us from evil.
For the kingdom, the power, and the glory are yours,
now and forever. Amen.

◆ ◆ ◆

In both instances the service continues with the following. All may stand.

Minister: The Lord bless you and watch over you.
The Lord be kind and gracious to you.
The Lord look favorably on you and give you peace.

—Numbers 6:24–25, adapt.

All: **Amen.**

The couple may exchange a kiss and may exchange greetings with the assembly, saying, "The peace of the Lord be with you." The act may conclude with the singing of a doxology or hymn and/or other music while the couple, their families, and other attendants recess.

Chapter Eight

Dedication and Consecration

Including:

A Liturgy for Groundbreaking

A Liturgy for Cornerstone Laying

A Liturgy for Dedication and Consecration
Including a Liturgy for Eucharist

A Liturgy for Mortgage Burning

A Liturgy for the Blessing of a Home
Including a Liturgy for Eucharist in the Home

Generally the acts of blessing we shall consider in this chapter are called "dedications." However, the dedication aspect is but one part of the act. "Dedication" is essentially what happens on the human side, namely, the setting apart of something by human intention for a specific purpose. In the process of constructing a new church building or making major renovations to an existing building or even in providing for some major physical appointment in a building, there is the act of dedicating, that is, making an offering of some tangible thing to God in the hope that God will use this for God's purposes. Yet more is intended than simply what happens on the human side. There is also a need for this physical thing to be blessed by God, as something that can be seen and used, as something that is kept as sacred by the community. "Consecration" is the act of setting apart as holy, a sacralizing by divine doing that marks something as sacred, that is, blessed by God and set apart *by God* for holy purposes. Although the dedication/consecration acts are focused on the physical thing being dedicated and consecrated, nevertheless, as in the blessing of bread and wine in the Eucharist and water in baptism,

109

the blessing is not alone of the physical thing itself but also the blessing of those who will be using whatever is blessed. A consecrated building without consecrated people isn't consecrated. Former church buildings can become restaurants — physically — but I have difficulties eating in restaurants that were formerly churches. My mind starts wandering and wondering about what happened to the people who once made this a church.

Four of the five acts in this chapter are liturgies of blessing to mark four stages in the building or renovation of a public place used by a Christian community. Each involves blessings directed to God by the assembly in praise and thanksgiving for God's wisdom and guidance in the planning and construction of the physical building(s) and the assembly's asking God to bless the various stages of the undertaking and, eventually, to consecrate the building(s) as a holy place for God's dwelling. We can see the first two essentially as preparatory acts for the third, namely, the final consecration of the building. The third, with some modification, may also be used for the consecration of major appointments at a time other than at the consecration of the building itself. The fourth, "A Liturgy for Mortgage Burning," is one that seldom appears in books of occasional services yet is the one for which I receive the most requests for help. It can mark a time of transition in which the congregation can begin to focus their efforts on some other aspect of ministry and mission. All four presuppose that they will be parts of regular services of Word and Sacrament. Suggestions for where they may be most appropriately included are indicated in the rubrics. "The Liturgy for Dedication and Consecration" includes an optional order for the Eucharist.

The fifth service is a liturgy for the blessing of a home. Sometimes these acts are called "house blessings." However, such a ritual of blessing is more than an act to sacralize a physical piece of real estate that may be inhabited by an individual or family for a certain length of time. No "house" is to be blessed by itself; the blessing makes sense only inasmuch as the "household," that is, those who live in it, also are blessed. The house itself is only the shell in which the household lives. Hence, I have chosen to call this the "blessing of a home" thereby to indicate that it is both the place itself as well as those who dwell in the house who are to blessed.

Although the home — and it may be a single house, an apartment, a condominium — is a "private" residence of a member or family in the faith community, the act of blessing nevertheless involves the community. Generally it may be the pastor who is the officiant in such a blessing act, but wouldn't it be far more meaningful if several other members of that community were invited to share in the act of blessing another's home?

This service also includes an optional liturgy for the Eucharist. The unison prayers before and after communion are shaped by an old German metrical table grace. It may be spoken or sung to the tune OLD HUNDREDTH. Scholars believe that the first Eucharistic meals were held in homes and that the prayers that eventually emerged as the Eucharistic prayer and post-communion thanksgiving prayer had their origin in table graces, one before the meal and one after the meal, as is still the practice in certain traditions.

In order for these liturgies to become more than monologues by the officiant, worship folders and bulletins need to be prepared — even for a house blessing. These are corporate acts of worship of a Christian community, and, in order for the community to do the worship work, they need some tools to be about it. Therefore, all these liturgies are included on the accompanying CD-ROM. Each includes many rubrics for the planning for and leadership of the services. These may be deleted or modified when the worship folders or bulletins are prepared. However, a separate script needs to be prepared for the leaders.

A LITURGY FOR
GROUNDBREAKING
CD-ROM 8.1.1

The assembly may process from the current place of worship to the place where the ground-breaking will occur, or they may gather at the site itself. Instrumental music may accompany the procession and the gathering. A large wooden cross may be carried in the procession or placed at the site prior to the gathering. Soil should be loosened so that adults and children may participate in breaking the ground. At the appropriate time, the blowing of a conch shell three times may call the assembly to worship.

Leader: This is the day that the Lord has made.

All: Let us rejoice and be glad in it.   — Psalm 118:24

The Taizé Gloria in Excelsis may be sung a cappella several times as a round or in unison.

Leader: Unless the Lord builds the house,

All: those who build it labor in vain.   — Psalm 127:1

Leader: Let us pray.
        With joy we come to this day, O God,
        to mark with the sign of the cross
        the place where a new _____ will be built.
        We come deeply aware that our plans and vision are of naught,
        unless they are your will for us.
        We confess our own finitude
        and acknowledge that whatever we build
        is but temporary in your sight.
        Yet in the imaginations of our hearts
        we dare to dream dreams of the future
        to which you are calling us.
        We are bold to believe that what we envision here
        may be an offering that will be well-pleasing to you.
        Bless this ground, we pray,
        that from it may emerge a new _____ ,
        consecrated as the place of your abiding with us,
        and dedicated to your mission of justice and reconciliation.
        Bless those who will build upon this ground;
        may their work be a gift to your honor and praise.
        And bless us in breaking ground for this new beginning,
        that we ourselves may be built into a spiritual house,
        worthy of your indwelling;

All: **Through Jesus Christ, the first and the last,**
        the beginning and the end.
        Amen.

Reader: A reading from Paul's first letter to the Corinthians.
        Listen to what the Spirit is saying to the churches.

1 Corinthians 3:6–7, 10–11 is read.

Reader: The Word of the Lord.

All: **Thanks be to God.**

Leader: As Abraham and Sarah set out in faith to a new land,
        by faith in the Triune God we *turn this sod/break this ground,*
        that here God will bring a new _____ into being,
        to God's glory and for the building up of the body of Christ.

As the first spadefuls are turned, a hymn or doxology may be sung. Children may be given toy shovels and encouraged to dig in the soil.

All pray the Lord's Prayer.

The service continues:

Leader: God asks us through the prophet Isaiah:
"I am about to do a new thing;
now it springs forth, do you not perceive it?"

All: *shouting*
Yes, Lord! Hallelujah!

The assembly may respond by singing several times, even with clapping, the chorus of the African American spiritual:

All: **Amen, Amen, Amen, Amen, Amen.**

Leader: The grace of the Lord Jesus Christ,
the love of God,
and the communion of the Holy Spirit be with you all.

All: **Amen.**

Leader: Go in peace to serve the Lord.

All: **Thanks be to God.**

A LITURGY FOR
CORNERSTONE LAYING
CD-ROM 8.2.1

The assembly may gather at the place where the cornerstone will be placed. Portable musical instruments may provide gathering music and accompaniment to the singing. The pealing of handbells may call the assembly to worship. Any announcements/directions should be given prior to the ringing of the bells so that the leader may begin immediately after the peals with:

Leader 1: Come to Christ, the living stone,
though rejected by mortals yet chosen and precious in God's sight,
and like living stones, let yourselves be built into a spiritual house,
to be a holy priesthood, to offer spiritual sacrifices
acceptable to God through Jesus Christ.

Leader 2: For it stands in scripture:
"See, I am laying in Zion a stone,
a cornerstone chosen and precious;
The stone that the builders rejected
has become the very head of the corner." — 1 Peter 2:4–7, adapt.

All: **For no one can lay any foundation
other than the one that has been laid;
that foundation is Jesus Christ.** — 1 Corinthians 3:11

All may sing: REGENT SQUARE

> **Christ is made the sure foundation,**
> **Christ the head and cornerstone,**
> **Chosen of our God and precious,**
> **binding all the church in one;**
> **Holy Zion's help forever,**
> **and our confidence alone.**
>
> **To this place where we are gathered,**
> **come, O Lord of Hosts, today;**
> **With your constant loving-kindness**
> **hear your people as they pray,**
> **and your fullest benediction**
> **shed within these walls always.**

Words: Latin, 6th–8th century, trans. John Mason Neale, 1851, alt.

Leader: Let us pray.
We cannot lay any other foundation, O God,
or place any other cornerstone
than that which already you have laid for us
in Christ Jesus, our Lord.
What we place today *at this corner/in this central place*
is but an outward symbol of what you already have given us
in the life, death, and resurrection of our Lord Jesus Christ.
So we ask you to build upon the foundation you have laid
and to establish a household upon this stone.
May what shall be completed here become a dwelling place for you,
acceptable and well-pleasing in your sight,
and a household in which people's lives
are grounded and shaped in the faith and love of Jesus Christ.

All: **Amen.**

Leader: Listen for the Word of God in a reading from Luke.

Luke 6:47–49 is read.

Leader: The Word of the Lord.

All: **Thanks be to God.**

Symbolic documents may be placed in the cornerstone, and brief remembrances and testimonies may be given.

Finally, water may be sprinkled from an evergreen bough on the stone and on those placing the stone, and as the stone is placed, the leader may pray:

Leader: Bless, O God, this cornerstone,
that it may be the foundation of faith in this place.
Bless and protect those who will build upon it.

All: **Bless us all, that we, like living stones,
may be built together spiritually into a holy temple,
worthy for the indwelling of your Holy Spirit. Amen.**

All may pray the Lord's Prayer.

Leader: Now to the One who by the power at work within us
is able to accomplish abundantly far more
than all we can ask or imagine,

All: **to God be glory in the church and in Christ Jesus
to all generations, forever and ever. Amen.**

— Ephesians 3:20–21, adapt.

Handbells may peal, and the service may conclude with the singing of a hymn and a final act of sending.

A LITURGY FOR DEDICATION AND CONSECRATION
CD-ROM 8.3.1

The assembly may gather outside the space to be dedicated and consecrated. The doors to the space shall be closed prior to the assembly's gathering.

A musical fanfare by instrumentalists or the blowing of a conch shell may call the assembly to worship.

A church official, either of the judicatory or the local church, shall knock on the door three times and say:

Official: Open to me the gates of righteousness,
that I may enter through them
and give thanks to the Lord.   — Psalm 118:19

A local church leader opens the door(s). Keys may be handed to the official or to another local church leader who says:

Leader: Peace be to this house, and to all who enter here.   — Luke 10:5, adapt.

All: **I was glad when they said to me,
Let us go into the house of the Lord.**   — Psalm 122:1, adapt.

The procession may move into the space to be consecrated. Throughout the procession the assembly may sing a cappella, repeated many times:

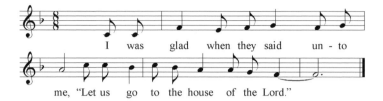

Words: Psalm 122:1, adapt.; Music: F. Russell Mitman, 2006

If this order is used for the consecration of a sanctuary, the Bible, a pitcher of water, and a chalice may be carried by representatives of the congregation. The procession may be preceded by a crucifer and acolyte(s). Each object is carried to its respective place — the pitcher to the font, the chalice to the table, and the Bible to the pulpit, yet each remains in the hands of those who carried them. The assembly may be directed by ushers to find seats. Vocal or instrumental music may accompany the processional. After all are assembled, the leader continues with hands uplifted:

Leader: How lovely is your dwelling place, O Lord of Hosts!

All: **My soul longs, indeed it faints for the courts of the Lord.**
            My heart and my flesh sing for joy to the living God.

Leader: Happy are those who live in your house, O God,
            ever singing your praise.   — Psalm 84:1–2, 4, adapt.

A hymn of praise may be sung.

Leader: Let us pray.

For the Dedication of a Building

Leader: Even heaven and the highest heaven cannot contain you, O God,
            much less this *house/place* that we have built!
            Yet in deep awareness of our own human frailty
            and the finiteness of whatever we do and make,
            we ask you humbly to accept this offering of our work and gifts.
            Receive this place we *dedicate/rededicate* for your dwelling
            and for the welcome of all who seek you here.
            Hear the prayers that your servants pray to you today,
            that your eyes may be open night and day toward this house,
            the place of which you said, "My name shall be there."
                                              — paraphrased from 1 Kings 8:27–29

All: **Amen.**

Or for other Dedications

Leader: Almighty God, unto whom all hearts are open,
              all desires known, and from whom no secrets are hid,
              cleanse the thoughts of our hearts
              by the inspiration of your Holy Spirit,
              that we may perfectly love you,
              and worthily magnify your holy name;
              through Christ our Lord.

All: **Amen.**   *—Book of Common Prayer,* adapt.

If this order is used for the consecration of a space other than a sanctuary, Psalm 122 may be chanted a cappella or spoken responsively or in unison.

If this order is used for the consecration of a sanctuary, the font, pulpit, and table may be dedicated according to the following:

Font: As water is poured into the font, the leader says:

Leader: We have been buried with Christ by baptism,
              so that, just as Christ was raised from the dead,
              so we too might walk in newness of life.   *—Romans 6:4, adapt.*

All: **We dedicate this font to the worship of the Triune God,**
              that here many may be washed in baptism
              and engrafted into the body of Christ.

Pulpit: As the Bible is placed on the pulpit, the leader says:

Leader: Jesus said, "If you continue in my word, you are truly my disciples;
              and you will know the truth, and the truth will make you free."
                                            —John 8:31–32

All: **We dedicate this pulpit to the worship of the Triune God,**
              that here the Word of God through the Scriptures will be heard
              and the good news of God in Christ rightly proclaimed.

Table: As the chalice is placed on the table, the leader says:

Leader: When Jesus was at the table with them, he took bread,
              blessed and broke it, and gave it to them.
              Then their eyes were opened, and they recognized him.
                                   —Luke 24:30–31, adapt.

All: **We dedicate this table to the worship of the Triune God,**
              that here, through broken bread and outpoured wine,
              we may feast with the risen Christ
              and know his presence with us.

Other appointments may be dedicated in a similar fashion; however, they are secondary to font, pulpit, and table. The assembly responds to each dedication with: "We dedicate this _____ to the worship of the Triune God."

The hymn by Fred Pratt Green "God Is Here! As We Your People Meet" may be sung. After all appointments have been dedicated, the leader continues:

Leader: Lift up your hearts!

All: We lift them up to the Lord!

Leader(s): *Each with hands uplifted*

Leader 1: We lift our hands and hearts to you, O God,
             in thanksgiving for all the gifts of your creation:
             For those who have seen visions
             and dreamed dreams of how this _____
             will enable your mission to be accomplished here,
             and for those who have given of their time, talent,
             and treasure to make it possible,

All: We thank you, O God.

Leader 2: For the materials of the earth
             that have provided for the fashioning of this _____,
             and for the skills and crafts with which you have endowed
             those who have been the designers and builders.

All: We thank you, O God.

If this is a memorial:

Leader: For _____, whose faithful generosity
             and dedication to your church we celebrate and remember,
             and for all the saints by whom we now are surrounded
             as a great cloud of witnesses,

All: We thank you, O God.

Leader 3: O God, the Source of every blessing,
             we now give this _____ to you,
             for your ministry and mission in this place,
             and for all who will be touched by the witness
             of this community of faith—
             through Word and Sacrament,
             Gospel hospitality and Christian formation,
             compassionate caring and reconciling love.

**All: Bless us and consecrate this _____
             that it may be sanctified by you and sacred to us,
             to your glory and for building up the body of Christ.**

A doxology or hymn may be sung.

The service continues with the reading of Scripture and the preaching of a sermon or homily. Suggested texts are:

> 1 Kings 8:22–23, 27b–30 (for consecration of a building)
> 2 Samuel 6:12–15, 17–19
> 1 Corinthians 3:1–11, 16–17 or Revelation 21:2–7
> Matthew 7:24–27 or Matthew 21:10–14

A creed or statement of faith may follow the sermon or homily, and the assembly may offer prayers of intercession concluding with (if Eucharist is celebrated):

Leader: Come, Holy One, come, and prepare our hearts
as we set the table for this holy feast
with the gifts of your creation and the offerings of our lives.

All: Amen.

The offering is received, and during the presentation of the gifts, including the bread and wine for the Eucharist, the congregation may stand and sing:

KREMSER

**We praise you, O God, our Redeemer, Creator,
In grateful devotion our tribute we bring.
We lay it before you, we kneel and adore you,
We bless your holy name, glad praises we bring.**

**With voices united our praises we offer,
To you, great Jehovah, glad anthems we raise;
Your strong arm will guide us, our God is beside us;
To you, our great Redeemer, forever be praise!**

Words: Julia C. Cory, 1902, alt.

Minister: The grace of the Lord Jesus Christ, the love of God,
and the communion of the Holy Spirit be with you.

All: And also with you.

The assembly may stand.

Minister: Let us give thanks to the Triune God.

All: It is right to give our thanks and praise.

Minister: At your call creation was birthed out of chaos
and by your breath the world and all living things came into being
and continually are sustained.

All: Receive, O God, our thanks and praise.

Minister: At your call Moses led your people from slavery to freedom,
and people of all ages, tongues, and races
are brought from bondage to the day of promise.

All: **Receive, O God, our thanks and praise.**

Minister: At your call prophets and apostles recall people and nations
from aimlessness and sin to the daylight of justice and righteousness,
and you offer the world new ways to reconciliation and peace.

All: **Receive, O God, our thanks and praise.**

Minister: In Christ you became flesh of our flesh and dwelt among humankind,
calling the world continually to glimpse your glory.

All: **Receive, O Christ, our thanks and praise.**

Minister: In Christ you suffered the humiliation of the cross
and triumphed in his resurrection,
calling all people from the tombs of death to the garden of new life.

All: **Receive, O Christ, our thanks and praise.**

Minister: In Christ you call the world to repentance
and offer to all who turn to him
the power to become children of God.

All: **Receive, O Christ, our thanks and praise.**

Minister: Through the Holy Spirit you call the church to faithful discipleship,
summoning men and women, youth and children,
to take up the cross and follow where Christ will lead.

All: **Receive, O Holy Spirit, our thanks and praise.**

Minister: Through the Holy Spirit you call ordinary people to mission and ministry,
empowering them with the gifts to preach, to teach, and to heal
in the name of Jesus.

All: **Receive, O Holy Spirit, our thanks and praise.**

Minister: Through the Holy Spirit you touch people
with sacred signs and seals,
calling the world from a secular numbness
into a holiness that is heaven's gift.

All: **Receive, O Holy Spirit, our thanks and praise.**

Minister: With the church on earth in communion with all the saints,
we sing our thanks and praise, calling on your holy name:

All: *singing*   NICAEA

> **Holy, holy, holy, Lord God Almighty!**
> **All your works shall praise your name in earth and sky and sea;**
> **Holy, holy, holy! merciful and mighty!**
> **God in three Persons, blessed Trinity!**

> Words: Reginald Heber, 1827, adapt.

If Eucharist is celebrated, the service continues with the following. If not, the service concludes with the ascription, "Behold, now the dwelling of God is with mortals..." and a hymn and blessing.

Eucharist
CD-ROM 8.3.2

Minister: Bless us, holy God, at this table,
                and bless these gifts of bread and wine that we offer you,
                offerings from your creation to feed us with the means of grace.
                Set them apart from their ordinary to a sacred and mystical use
                that they may be to us the body and blood of Christ,
                and that here we may eat and drink with Christ
                and all the saints in glory everlasting. Amen.

All: **Christ has died, Christ is risen, and Christ will come again!**

The minister breaks the bread and pours the cup while reciting the words of institution. All pray the Lord's Prayer.

Minister: *administering the bread* The bread of heaven given for you.

Each person: Amen.

Minister: *administering the cup* The cup of salvation shed for you.

Each person: Amen.

After all have been served the service continues with the following thanksgiving:

Minister: Holy God, we rejoice that you have fed us at this table
                with the spiritual food of the body and blood of Christ,
                and have united us in communion
                with your church on earth and in heaven.
                Grant us the abiding presence of your Holy Spirit.
                Enrich our faith.
                Nourish us through the means of grace.
                Strengthen our life together.
                Confirm us in our ministry and mission.
                And with glad and generous hearts,
                may we praise you and find favor with all people,
                to the honor and glory of Jesus Christ.

All: **Amen.**

Leader: Behold, now the dwelling of God is with mortals. God will dwell with
           them as their God; they will be God's peoples, and God will be with them.
                                                          — Revelation 21:3, adapt.

All: **Blessing and glory and wisdom and thanksgiving**
           and honor and power and might
           be to our God forever and ever!
           Amen and amen!   — Revelation 7:12, adapt.

The service may conclude with a hymn and a blessing.

A LITURGY FOR
MORTGAGE BURNING
CD-ROM 8.4.1

*This act takes place after the sermon and the prayers of the people. Depending on the fire
codes, the assembly may process to an out-of-doors space for this ritual. A small table-top
brazier as used for charcoal fires may be used — without charcoal, of course. If this liturgy
is used out of doors, the assembly may gather around the brazier. Instrumental music may
accompany the procession.*

*A representative of the congregation carries the mortgage certificate on a tray. Another person
may carry a pot with burning incense. A third person carries the brazier. A fourth person
carries a lighted candle.*

Reader: A reading from the prophet Isaiah.
           Isaiah 6:1–8 is read.

Reader: The Word of the Lord.

All: **Thanks be to God.**

Leader: In (*date*) _____ a mortgage was signed
           to pay for _____ .
           That mortgage now has been satisfied
           through the many gifts of many people
           who have committed themselves and their resources
           to this project.
           It is in humble and heartfelt gratitude that we gather today
           to submit this mortgage certificate to a consuming fire,
           that its financial burden be lifted from us,
           and that with joy and thanksgiving we mark the completion
           of this project.

*An acolyte may light a taper from a paschal or other candle and bring the flame to the
leader. Those bearing the tray with the mortgage certificate and the pot of burning incense
join the leader at the brazier.*

Leader: Let us pray.
          Holy God, who came to Moses in a burning bush,
          come to us in this flame of fire and mark this place as holy ground.
          Here we hold in sacred remembrance the sacrifices
          of all who have given so generously to fulfill this commitment.
          As your servant Isaiah was touched
          by a burning coal from the altar
          and he and his people were cleansed,
          so let the flame of your Holy Spirit now burn away this debt,
          that we may be set free for the ministry and mission
          to which you call us, and be given wisdom and courage
          for the living of these days.

The leader ignites the mortgage certificate with the flame from the taper.

Leader: O God, set our hearts ablaze with desire to do your will
          and, when you call us in Jesus Christ, empower us to respond:

All: **Here am I; send me.**

All: *singing*   ST. MATTHEW

          O Spirit of the Living God, O Light and Holy Fire,
          Descend upon your church once more, our dreams and hopes inspire.
          Fill us with love and joy and power, with righteousness and peace,
          Till Christ shall dwell in human hearts and sin and sorrow cease.
          Words: Henry Hallam Tweedy, 1933, alt.

During the singing of the hymn the assembly may return to their places. The service continues
with the offertory and Eucharist.

A LITURGY FOR THE BLESSING OF A HOME
INCLUDING A LITURGY FOR EUCHARIST
IN THE HOME
CD-ROM 8.5.1

All may gather at the door. The leader may dip an evergreen branch into a bowl of water
and sprinkle water on the door and on those gathered as he or she says:

Leader 1: Peace be to this house and to all who enter it!
                                                    — paraphrased from Luke 10:5

All: **Amen.**

Leader 2: Unless the Lord builds the house,

All: **those who build it labor in vain.**   — Psalm 127:1

The door is opened and all gather inside the door.

Leader 1: Jesus said,
           "Those who love me will keep my word,
           and my Father will love them,
           and we will come to them and make our home with them."

                                       —John 14:23, adapt.

Householder:
           As for me and my household, we will serve the Lord.

All: **Thanks be to God.**   —Joshua 24:15

A candle may be lighted and presented to a member of the household.

Leader 1: This is the message we have heard from God and proclaim to you,
           that God is light and in God there is no darkness at all.

                                    —1 John 1:5, adapt.

Leader 2: Let us pray.
           O God of light, continue to shed your light throughout this home,
           that all who live here and all who find hospitality here
           may dwell in the radiance of your presence;
           through Jesus Christ, the Light of the world.

All: **Amen.**

The assembly moves to a living room or family room.

Leader 1: Jesus said,
           "Where two or three are gathered in my name,
           there am I in the midst of them."   —Matthew 18:20, RSV

A cross or house blessing certificate may be placed on the wall.

Leader 2: Let us pray.
           Lord Jesus, be present in this household,
           not only as the holy guest but also as the extravagant host,
           welcoming all who gather here, without distinction,
           into the warm embrace of your reconciling and redeeming love.

All: **Amen.**

The assembly moves to the kitchen or dining room.

Leader 1: All your works shall give thanks to you, O Lord,

All: **and all your faithful shall bless you.**

Leader 1: The eyes of all look to you,
           and you give them their food in due season.

All: **You open your hand, satisfying the desire of every living thing.**

                                —Psalm 145:10, 15–16, adapt.

Leader 2: You fill your people, O God, with good things —
good things to feed and nourish the body,
good things to satisfy the longing of the soul.
Bless those who prepare food
and bless those who eat it,
that, as Jesus on the day of resurrection
broke bread with two disciples, all who gather here
may have their eyes opened and recognize him
as a holy presence at this table.

All: **Amen.**

The assembly may move to a bedroom.

Leader 1: Let the light of your face shine on us, O Lord!

All: **You have put gladness in my heart,**
more than when grain and wine abound.

Leader 1: I will both lie down and sleep in peace;

All: **for you alone, O Lord, make me lie down in safety.** — Psalm 4:6b–8

Leader 2: Sanctify, O God, our lying down and our rising up,
that, whether asleep or awake, we may be kept in your care
and always refreshed by your renewing grace.

All: **Amen.**

All may return to the dining room or kitchen and sit around the table. The lighted candle
may be placed on the table. Bread and wine may be brought to the table for Eucharist.

If Eucharist is not celebrated, the liturgy concludes in the living room with the reading from
John's Gospel and the final blessing.

Eucharist
CD-ROM 8.5.2

Minister: The Lord be with you.

All: **And also with you.**

Minister: Lift up your hearts.

All: **We lift them to the Lord.**

Minister: Let us give thanks to the Lord our God.

All: **It is right to give our thanks and praise.**

Minister: We remember, O God, that from the beginning
you have called your people together
into the household of faith

and have bound us together
with the signs and seals of your everlasting covenant.

We rejoice that in Jesus Christ,
and through the one offering of himself,
we who are buried and raised with him in baptism
are incorporated into his body
and made living members of his church.

By the blessing of your Holy Spirit
sanctify us and this bread and wine,
that we may be nourished through these holy mysteries,
and strengthened for service in the name of Jesus Christ.

All: **Amen.**

The minister repeats the words of institution while breaking the bread and pouring the cup. Intercessions may be offered. All pray the Lord's Prayer followed by:

All: *speaking or singing* OLD HUNDREDTH

Come, Jesus, Lord, and be our guest
To share with us communion blest;
And with this bread and wine impart
Your grace to every waiting heart.

The communion may be distributed or shared with appropriate words of administration. After all have received, the service continues with the following.

Minister: Let us give thanks.

All: *speaking or singing* OLD HUNDREDTH

We thank you, Lord, for holy food:
Our Christ's own body, his own blood,
The Bread of Life, the Branches' Vine,
To feed and nourish humankind.

May be added: "Praise God from whom all blessings flow...."

With or without the celebration of Eucharist the service continues:

Leader 1: Jesus said,
"Abide in me as I abide in you.
Just as the branch cannot bear fruit by itself
unless it abides in the vine,
neither can you unless you abide in me.
I am the vine, you are the branches.
Those who abide in me and I in them bear much fruit,
because apart from me you can do nothing." —John 15:4–5

Leader 2: Let us pray.
Bless this house, O God,
and sanctify those who dwell here,
that this may be a home for you,
a dwelling place for your abiding.

All: **Amen.**

Leader 1: *addressing the members of the household:*
The Lord is your keeper;
The Lord will keep your life.
The Lord will keep your going out and your coming in
from this time on and forevermore.   —Psalm 121:5a, 7b, 8, adapt.

Leader 1: *addressing all:*
The peace of the Lord Jesus Christ be with you.

All: **And also with you.**

The assembly may exchange expressions of peace.

Chapter Nine

Anointing for Healing

Including:

A Liturgy for Anointing for Healing

A Liturgy for Eucharist in a Service of Anointing

A Liturgy for Penitence in a Service of Anointing

A Liturgy for Anointing and Holy Communion with Individuals

Since my first publication of a liturgy for healing in 1987, significant developments have taken place in the church's rediscovery of the place of services of anointing for healing in the liturgical life of congregations. It was a deeply spiritual physician and elder in a congregation I served who came to me some thirty years ago and said, "Russ, I think we need to have services for healing in this church." The theological environment in which I had been trained had no room for such things. We took seriously Jesus' teaching and preaching ministries, but, as Thomas Jefferson did with his Bible, we cut out the accounts of Jesus' ministry of healing and the attendant miracle stories. From the lofty perches of a leftover Enlightenment rationalism we jokingly left what we called "faith healing" up to the TV evangelists and itinerant revivalists. When that elder, whose medical competence and advice I trusted and followed, came to me with his request for healing services, I had to do a lot of reading and reflection. I also needed to be converted theologically and spiritually to rediscover what I had overlooked or abandoned in my own previous theological and spiritual pilgrimage — and in the educational programs of those who trained me for ministry. Or perhaps I was mentally or physically absent when such things were discussed.

There were few liturgical resources to help that congregation and me on our journey. The 1977 revision of *The Book of Common Prayer* of the Episcopal Church with its liturgy for "Ministration to the Sick" had not

128

yet been published. There was some significant theological work being done in Roman Catholic circles, arising out of its traditional sacraments of penance and unction, which had become pretty much "last rites" administrations. It was the seminal work of Morton Kelsey, whose own spiritual journey so much paralleled my own, that brought me to a new perspective on the stories of healing in the New Testament and a new understanding of the ministry of healing in the church. So the physician-elder and I preached a dialogue sermon to introduce a holistic perspective to healing, and the leaders of that congregation and I began to shape a liturgy for healing that eventually made its way into the first edition of liturgies entitled *Worship Vessels: Resources for Renewal* that was published in 1987. We had little to borrow from, for most denominational books of worship and hymnals that now include services for healing were still in the writing and editing stages. The liturgy of anointing for healing included here is what has evolved over the past thirty years both in the liturgical experiences of that congregation and in subsequent settings to which I have been called to ministry and in which anointing services are normative both in intimate gatherings as well as in large assemblies.

In the congregation in which this all began, we saw the rites for healing as natural extensions of the church's ministry as intercessors, and the services of anointing were integrated into services of Word and Sacrament, first on an occasional basis and then monthly. Most often when people came forward to receive the anointing and laying on of hands, they did so not for themselves but for others. In that sense, they became a community of healers. I still remember with tears when one of the elders, a man of considerable wealth with a trucking empire that stretched across the nation, knelt down and said, "I come to receive laying on of hands for a young man who washes our trucks and recently was diagnosed with lymphoma." I thought that when I left that congregation for another pastoral call they would no longer continue the practice of monthly anointing services, but they did not cease, and almost twenty years later that congregation still includes the rite for healing monthly as part of the services of Word and Sacrament. It has become integrally a part of who they are as a Christian congregation.

The following liturgy of anointing for healing is designed to be an extension of intercessory prayers in services of Word and Sacrament. It may take place immediately following the prayers of intercession before the offertory. If the accompanying liturgy for the celebration of the Eucharist is to be included, the offertory serves as a bridge between the two.

If Eucharist is not to be celebrated, the service continues with the Lord's Prayer, the final exhortation, a hymn or doxology, and a blessing.

However, there are occasions when a congregation may wish to schedule a separate service of anointing. Sometimes such an approach is less threatening initially to those who have not yet made the theological and spiritual pilgrimage necessary to accept and to appreciate services for healing. If this liturgy is used in such a separate service, the order leading up to where this liturgy begins should include the normative elements, according to the classic *ordo* of Christian worship: some gathering/penitential act(s) followed by the reading of Scripture texts, the preaching of a sermon or homily, and prayers of the people. These parts of the service should be shaped by texts that are appointed or chosen and that focus on God's intention for the wholeness of creation and Jesus' ministry of healing. Such texts may include, but do not need to be restricted to: James 5:14–16; Psalm 23; Mark 6:7, 12–13, 53–56. These particular texts are appointed for several Sundays in the three-year cycle of the *Revised Common Lectionary*. Such Sundays can become occasions to introduce a rite for healing either in a regular weekend service or within a special service. Of course, there are many more texts in the three-year cycle of the lectionary that recount Jesus' healing ministry and the healing ministry of the early Christian community. These can become the occasions for the shaping of services of anointing for healing in the regular times when Christians assemble.

Congregations need to encounter again what is so central to faith shaped by the biblical witness and by traditions of the church that, sadly, have been forgotten or ignored, particularly in Protestant Enlightenment thinking. We have do here not with "last ditch" measures and miracle "cures" that run contrary to medical science but with a therapy (*therapeuo* is one of the words used for healing in the New Testament) that is in harmony with the most sophisticated of medical technologies and therapies. That was the approach that my elder-physician and I took some thirty years ago. Nor is the intention of a liturgy of anointing for healing to focus on the person performing a healing rite. Jesus never allowed the attention to focus on himself as healer but always focused the recipients — and the audience — on the God who is the source of healing and wholeness. Healing, to Jesus, was a sign that the Kingdom or Reign of God was at hand. Therefore, in my mind, rites of healing, regardless of the settings, need to take the posture of prayer to guard against the kind of religious exhibitionism that has soured many of the faithful.

It is interesting that the secular world has begun to inquire into the phenomena of healings that have taken place outside the parameters of traditional medical practices and to investigate, even with the use of sophisticated medical and scientific technology, the role of faith in bringing people to wholeness. Perhaps it was that he experienced some realities that were outside the box of his own medical training that led that elder-physician to ask for services for healing thirty years ago. Even the curiosity of the media has been aroused to the connection between prayer and healing. Yet when we rediscover the traditions from which we have come, the church has understood the connection ever since it began retelling and writing down the stories of Jesus' healings and the early church's experience of the healing power of God in Jesus Christ.

As the element in baptism is water and the elements in the Eucharist are bread and wine, in the rite of anointing the element is oil, generally some kind of vegetable oil, most often olive oil. Oil in ancient times was one of those common everyday staples of living. In addition to the use of oil in the Old Testament as an agent in conferring authority, the use of oil as a healing unction was common medical practice. And it is natural for such an ordinary thing to become a sign of something extraordinary — namely, in the New Testament a sign of God's healing power. So when Jesus sent out the Twelve in mission, Mark records, "They cast out many demons, and anointed with oil many who were sick and cured them" (Mark 6:13). The pastoral letter of James asks, "Are any among you sick? They should call for the elders of the church and have them pray over them, anointing them with oil in the name of the Lord" (James 5:14).

Anointing, although tradition has related it to the healing of physical disease, need not be restricted to those who are sick. Anointing with oil also can be a marker of thanksgiving and joy, as in "the oil of gladness" of Isaiah 61:3. It can be part of the sending act, namely, as a commissioning (with or without the sign of the cross) to empower members of the assembly to carry on Christ' mission beyond the walls of the sanctuary.

The oil has no magical power of its own; it simply is an outward and visible element that becomes by the power of God, when it is joined with prayer and administered by and to people, an unction of sacramental dimensions. Protestant minds would not call such anointing a sacrament, yet one could ask the irreverent question: Did the reformers of the sixteenth century overlook some things in their numbering and defining of things sacramental?

Anointing with oil is joined with the act of laying on of hands. This is another one of those acts of blessing that have been part of the church's experience: in baptism, confirmation, ordination, marriage, and intercessory prayer. The touching has no magical power in itself. Rather, it becomes a sign of the healing touch of Jesus Christ mediated through human touch. Again, the secular therapeutic community knows the healing power of touch and trains persons in the therapeutic art of touching to relieve pain, particularly with patients in the terminal stages of life. Yet this act has been with us ever since Jesus laid on hands for healing. Mark records, "Jairus came and, when he saw him, fell at his feet and begged him repeatedly, 'My little daughter is at the point of death. Come and lay your hands on her, so that she may be made well, and live'" (Mark 5:22–23). Luke the physician says, "All those who had any who were sick with various kinds of diseases brought them to [Jesus] and he laid his hands on each of them and cured them" (Luke 4:40). Further, the act of laying on of hands by the disciple Ananias was what brought healing to Paul after his encounter on the road to Damascus that had left him blind: "Ananias . . . laid his hands on Saul and said, Brother Saul, the Lord Jesus, who appeared to you on your way here, has sent me so that you may regain your sight" (Acts 9:17). The wondrous news is that healing in the name of Jesus Christ did not stop at the crucifixion but is a ministry of the risen Christ handed over to the church for the church to lay on hands for healing. As Acts testifies, it worked! And it works!

Although there is a significant role for confession of sin in any service of worship — including services of anointing — we need to guard against the notion that one's suffering is the result of a moral flaw or lack of faith and, therefore, is God's punishment for sin. Yes, we all engage in behaviors that are inimical to health and wholeness, and we need to confess that we always miss the mark God intends for us. However, the age-old question, "Why, God, did you do this to . . . ?" still has a way of haunting the minds and souls of sufferers and their loved ones. There is a need for confession that is cathartic, but, as in the normal *ordo* of Christian worship, such penitential acts should occur *before* the reading of Scripture and preaching, so that the Word of God can become both a word of *forgiveness* and an *invitation* to prayers for healing. Hence, the liturgy that follows presupposes that a penitential act has preceded what begins here essentially as an extension of intercessory prayers occurring *after* Scripture and sermon. A liturgy for penitence and forgiveness that can be used as a prelude to the healing rite is also included here on page 137. Rites of anointing for healing are for wholeness and need to be part of the whole worship experience.

Most liturgies for healing and Eucharist are in settings of public worship. However, there are occasions when the church needs to· minister to individuals in settings other than the ones in which the community normally assembles. Sometimes these were referred to as "private communions," although, to me, those two words are contradictions in terms. There is no such thing as a "private" communion. If there is a need for Eucharist to be celebrated with an individual, the sheer presence of two or more people makes this a corporate experience. Often such ministrations are given to those confined to their homes or in institutions. An adaptation of the corporate liturgy for use with an individual is included on page 139, and anointing may be part of such a service.

In the following liturgy the word "minister" refers to anyone the congregation designates as the one(s) who administer(s). (Note the Latin roots: *ad*, "to," and *ministrare*, "minister.") Ministers may be the ordained ones, but the gift of healing is not restricted to those upon whom ordination has been conferred. Hands are laid on each of the baptized, commissioning all to be agents of healing. Each congregation has many healers, including children, who may assist in the prayers and in the administration of the rite in its corporate setting. Even in settings with individuals, it is important that these occasions be seen as extended ministries of the whole congregation. Appointed elders or deacons or other designated persons should accompany the pastor(s)/minister(s) in these visitations and liturgical acts.

A LITURGY FOR ANOINTING FOR HEALING
CD-ROM 9.1.1

Minister: Christ promises to reach out to all people with healing grace
and, through the Holy Spirit, endows the church
with many gifts to become instruments of healing
to all who hurt in body, in mind, and in spirit.
Upon this promise and commission,
the church is entrusted with the ministry of anointing
and laying on of hands, that through these signs
those who suffer may be in touch with the power that brings wholeness.

Therefore *I/we* now invite those who desire to receive
the *anointing/and/or/laying on of hands* for healing,
either for themselves or for others, to come forward

and to kneel or stand at the chancel or to sit in the front *pews/chairs*.
If you come that you may be a channel for others to receive healing,
please tell *us/me* the names of those persons.

All: *singing* WINCHESTER NEW

With healing hand be present, Lord,
that these to health may be restored;
To all who suffer turn your face
and touch them with anointing grace.

Words: F. Russell Mitman, 1985

And/Or

Minister: Gracious God, in Christ you have promised us wholeness.
Hear us now as we pray for all who are sick
in body and soul, mind and spirit, and especially for _____,
that *he/she/they* may be healed, through Jesus Christ. Amen.

If oil is to be used for anointing, the minister may pray the following prayer. If anointing
does not take place, the minister shall proceed to the act of laying on of hands.

Leader: Send down your Holy Spirit, O God, and sanctify this oil,
that, as the apostles anointed many who were sick and they were healed,
so also may it be a sign to us of the blessed unction from above. Amen.

Each minister dips a thumb into the oil and places it on the forehead of each person, with or
without making the sign of the cross.

Minister: _____, *I/we* anoint you with oil,
that the healing balm of God's mercy may comfort you
and relieve your suffering.

And/Or
The minister(s) may lay hands on each person.

Minister: _____, in the name of Jesus Christ *I/we* lay hands on you,
that the power of God working in *you/(Name[s])* _____,
will bring *you/him/her/them* to wholeness.

All: **Amen.**

The minister(s) may add:

Minister: To those who touched his garment
and were touched by his healing grace,
Jesus said, "Your faith has made you whole."

And/Or

Minister: With confidence in Christ's healing presence in your life,
arise and go in peace.

A hymn such as "My Shepherd Will Supply My Need," or "The Lord's My Shepherd," or a unison or responsive reading or singing of Psalm 23 may be included. The service continues with the offertory.

    If Eucharist is to be included, the service continues with the following:

A LITURGY FOR EUCHARIST
IN A SERVICE OF ANOINTING
CD-ROM 9.1.2

Minister: Come, bless the Lord!

All: **We lift up our hands to the holy place and bless the Lord!**
                                             —Psalm 134:1–2, adapt.

Minister: Holy God,
           we praise you for the wellsprings of your healing and restoring grace.
           We thank you for your never-failing goodness that relieves our weariness,
           anoints our fears, and fills us with good things.
           We rejoice that in Christ Jesus we are promised a new creation,
           and by his hand laid on us
           we are touched with his healing and resurrecting power.
           We marvel at the countless mysteries you work through your Holy Spirit
           and the variety of spiritual gifts with which you endow your people to
           bring others to wholeness.

All: **Holy, Holy, Holy, God Almighty!**
           The whole earth overflows with your glory!

Minister: We offer you these gifts of bread and wine,
           praying that by the transforming power of your Holy Spirit
           they may be to us a means of sharing
           in the very body and blood of Christ.

All: **Surely he has borne our griefs and carried our sorrows;**
           he was wounded for our transgressions,
           he was bruised for our iniquities;
           by the punishment he suffered we are healed,
           by the blows he received we are made whole.
                               —Isaiah 53:4–5, RSV, adapt.

Minister: As Jesus taught his disciples, we pray:

All: **Our Father in heaven:**
           Hallowed be your name,
           Your kingdom come,
           Your will be done, on earth as in heaven.

Give us today our daily bread.
Forgive us our sins, as we forgive those who sin against us.
Save us from the time of trial, and deliver us from evil.
For the kingdom, the power, and the glory are yours,
now and forever. Amen.

The minister repeats the words of institution while breaking the bread and pouring the cup.

Minister: *administering the bread*
(*Name*) _____,
this is the body of Christ, given for you.

Each person: Amen.

Minister: *administering the cup*
(*Name*) _____,
this is the blood of Christ, poured out for you.

Each person: Amen.

After all have communed, the service continues with the following thanksgiving. In services in which the Eucharist is not celebrated, the service continues with the offertory and the following thanksgiving. The setting of a portion of Psalm 103 may serve as a prayer of thanksgiving after the offering is received. No other prayer of dedication is necessary.

Minister: Bless the Lord, O my soul,

All: **and all that is within me, bless God's holy name.**

Minister: Bless the Lord, O my soul,

All: **and do not forget all God's benefits —**

Minister: It is God who forgives all your iniquity,
who heals all your diseases,
who redeems your life from the Pit,
who crowns you with steadfast love and mercy,
who satisfies you with good things,
so that your youth is renewed like the eagle's.

All: **Bless the Lord, O my soul.**   — Psalm 103:1–5, adapt.

Minister: Now to the One who by the power at work within us
is able to accomplish abundantly far more
than all we can ask or imagine,

All: **to God be glory in the church
and in Christ Jesus to all generations,
forever and ever. Amen.**   — Ephesians 3:20–21, adapt.

The service concludes with a hymn or doxology and a blessing.

A LITURGY FOR PENITENCE
IN A SERVICE OF ANOINTING
CD-ROM 9.2.1

The following gathering and penitential act is designed for a service in which the rite of anointing will take place. It should precede the reading of Scripture and the sermon or homily.

Minister: Our help is in the name of the Lord,

All: **Who made heaven and earth.**   —Psalm 124:8

Minister: Those who wait for the Lord shall renew their strength,
            they shall mount up with wings like eagles,
            they shall run and not be weary,
            they shall walk and not faint.   —Isaiah 40:31

The congregation may stand and sing a hymn or Psalm.

Minister: When we wait in the holy presence of God,
            we are conscious of the frailty of our human condition.
            When we encounter the presence of Christ the healer,
            we are aware of the sickness in our own souls and minds and bodies.
            Let us humble ourselves before God and confess the ways
            in which we have missed the mark God intends for us
            and ask for God's healing forgiveness in Christ Jesus.

The assembly may be seated or kneel. Ample time should be allowed after each petition. Each of the petitions may be spoken by a different person situated throughout the assembly.

Minister: God of health and wholeness,

All: **we come before you with deep wounds.**

Minister: Our lives are fractured by broken promises. *Silence*
            Our bodies are infected by bad habits and attitudes. *Silence*
            Our relationships are severed by supersensitive prides. *Silence*
            Our souls are battered by competing loyalties that vie for our
                allegiance. *Silence*
            Our emotions are calloused by devices we invent to protect ourselves
                from the cries of others and from our own inner anguish. *Silence*

Minister: O God, there is no health in us,

All: **yet we yearn for wholeness.**

A Kyrie or Psalm 130 may be said or sung in unison or responsively.

And/Or

A time for personal confession, silent or spoken aloud, may be offered, allowing for the catharsis of whatever it is that weighs heavily on the soul.

And/Or

A rite of footwashing or handwashing may be included here. A liturgy for washing appears on page 65.

The service continues with the following. The "Amen" may be sung or spoken. The biblical text in the words of forgiveness may be spoken by a second leader at some distance from the first one.

Minister: Forgive our sin and mend our brokenness,

All: **make of us a new creation
through the healing touch of Jesus Christ.
Amen.**

Minister: Listen to the comforting assurance of the grace of God,
          promised in the Gospel to all who turn to God and believe:

      God so loved the world that he gave his only Son,
      so that everyone who believes in him may not perish
      but may have eternal life.
      Indeed, God did not send the Son into the world to condemn the world,
      but in order that the world might be saved through him.

                              —John 3:16–17

      Sisters and brothers, believe the Good news!
      In Jesus Christ we are redeemed and forgiven!

All: *shouting*
Amen! Hallelujah!

A doxology or hymn of praise and thanksgiving may be sung. The service continues with the reading of Scripture and a sermon or homily.

A LITURGY FOR ANOINTING
AND HOLY COMMUNION WITH INDIVIDUALS
CD-ROM 9.3.1

The following adaptation of the liturgy of anointing and holy communion may be used for the anointing of an individual and/or for celebrating holy communion with those who cannot attend a service in the church.

Leader: Listen to the comforting assurance of our Lord Jesus Christ:
"Come to me, all you that are weary and are carrying heavy burdens,
and I will give you rest.
Take my yoke upon you, and learn from me;
for I am gentle and humble in heart, and you will find rest for your souls.
For my yoke is easy, and my burden is light."   —Matthew 11:28–30

Minister: Let us pray.
Gracious God, in Christ Jesus you have promised us wholeness.
Hear us now as we pray for all
who need your comforting and healing touch,
and especially for _____,
that *he/she/they* may know your presence with *him/her,*
through Jesus Christ. Amen.

Other intercessions for the individual and others may be offered.

If oil is to be used for anointing, the minister may pray the following prayer. If anointing does not take place, the minister shall proceed to the act of laying on of hands.

Minister: Send down your Holy Spirit, O God, and sanctify this oil,
that, as the apostles anointed many who were sick and they were healed,
so also may it be a sign to us of the blessed unction from above. Amen.

Each minister dips a thumb into the oil and places it on the forehead, with or without making the sign of the cross.

Minister: _____, *I/we* anoint you with oil,
that the healing balm of God's mercy may comfort you
and relieve your suffering.

And/Or

The minister(s) may lay hands on each person.

Minister: _____, in the name of Jesus Christ *I/we* lay hands on you,
that the power of God working in *you/(Name[s])* _____,
will bring *you/him/her/them* to wholeness.

All: **Amen.**

A reading of Psalm 23 may be included.

Minister: Holy God,
             we praise you for the wellsprings of your healing and restoring grace.
             We thank you for your never-failing goodness that relieves our weariness,
             anoints our fears, and fills us with good things.
             We rejoice that in Christ Jesus we are promised a new creation,
             and by his hand laid on us
             we are touched with his healing and resurrecting power.

             Holy, Holy, Holy, God Almighty!
             The whole earth overflows with your glory!

Minister: We offer you these gifts of bread and wine,
             praying that by the transforming power of your Holy Spirit
             they may be to us a means of sharing
             in the very body and blood of Christ.
             Surely he has borne our griefs and carried our sorrows;
             he was wounded for our transgressions,
             he was bruised for our iniquities;
             by the punishment he suffered we are healed,
             by the blows he received we are made whole.
                                               —Isaiah 53:4–5, RSV, adapt.

Minister: As Jesus taught his disciples, we pray:

*The Lord's Prayer may be prayed in any version or language or in the following ecumenical
version:*

All: **Our Father in heaven:**
               Hallowed be your name,
               Your kingdom come,
               Your will be done, on earth as in heaven.
               Give us today our daily bread.
               Forgive us our sins, as we forgive those who sin against us.
               Save us from the time of trial, and deliver us from evil.
               For the kingdom, the power, and the glory are yours,
               now and forever. Amen.

*The minister repeats the words of institution while breaking the bread and pouring the cup,
followed by:*

Minister: *administering the bread*
             (*Name*) _____,
             this is the body of Christ, given for you.

Minister: *administering the cup*
             (*Name*) _____,
             this is the blood of Christ, poured out for you.

After all have communed, the service continues with the following thanksgiving.

Leader: Let us give thanks
For the bread that, more than bread alone,
nourishes our bodies and feeds our souls
with food for eternal life,
For the wine that, poured out in your self-sacrifice for us,
refreshes our bodies and revives our souls,
Receive our thanks, O Christ.
Amen.

Minister: Now to the One who by the power at work within us
is able to accomplish abundantly far more
than all we can ask or imagine,
to God be glory in the church
and in Christ Jesus to all generations,
forever and ever. Amen.   —Ephesians 3:20–21, adapt.

Minister: The Lord bless you and keep you;
the Lord make his face to shine upon you, and be gracious to you;
the Lord lift up his countenance upon you, and give you peace.
Amen.   —Numbers 6:24–26

Chapter Ten

A Time of Dying

This chapter is about the final chapter in our lives, namely, our final passage from life to death. The liturgical rite that marks this time for those of us in the mainline of Protestantism is not a sacrament, yet it is an act that deserves to be honored as a paramount sacred moment. Too often many in our faith communities are allowed to die in the loneliness and sterility of medical institutions. Sometimes the final moments of one's life are not afforded the luxury of the presence of loved ones and of the church, and the final good-byes are left to a time of viewing of the body or of a memorial service. Whenever possible, I believe, it is the church's responsibility to minister to the dying, that is, *to bless* the dying in the assurances of the Christian faith, praying for them and anointing them with the signs and seals of God's promise of eternal life in Jesus Christ. In so doing, the church also is ministering to the loved ones who may be gathered with him or her.

Copies of this liturgy may be made from the accompanying CD-ROM and kept available when needed for times of dying in the life of the community. Sometimes, however, it may not be possible to have copies at hand for those gathered with the dying person. Thus, the liturgy may simply be used as one from a minister's manual without the responses of those assembled. However, they may be encouraged with simple instructions to respond with the "Amens" and to pray the Lord's Prayer and perhaps also the Twenty-third Psalm.

A LITURGY FOR
A TIME OF DYING
CD-ROM 10.1.1

Leader: The Lord be with you.

All: And also with you.

Leader: Let us pray.
            O God, our Alpha and Omega, our beginning and our end:
            look now with favor on your servant _____ .
            Bless *him/her* as *he/she* passes from life to death,
            and let the angels of your mercy carry *him/her* into your presence;
            through Christ our Lord.

All: Amen.

Leader: In Christ you were buried with him in baptism,
            and raised with him through the power of God.

—Colossians 2:2, adapt.

All: Thanks be to God.

Psalm 23 may be read or said in unison in any version or language, or in either of the
following translations:

> **The Lord is my shepherd; I shall not want.**
> **He makes me to lie down in green pastures;**
> **He leads me beside the still waters. He restores my soul;**
> **He leads me in the paths of righteousness for His name's sake.**
> **Yea, though I walk through the valley of the shadow of death,**
> **I will fear no evil; for You are with me;**
> **Your rod and Your staff, they comfort me.**
> **You prepare a table before me in the presence of my enemies;**
> **You anoint my head with oil; my cup runs over.**
> **Surely goodness and mercy shall follow me all the days of my life;**
> **And I will dwell in the house of the Lord forever.**
>> —The Holy Bible, New King James Version

> **The Lord is my shepherd, I shall not want;**
> **he makes me lie down in green pastures.**
> **He leads me beside still waters; he restores my soul.**
> **He leads me in paths of righteousness for his name's sake.**
> **Even though I walk through the valley of the shadow of death,**
> **I fear no evil; for thou art with me;**
> **thy rod and thy staff, they comfort me.**
> **Thou preparest a table before me in the presence of my enemies;**
> **thou anointest my head with oil, my cup overflows.**

Surely goodness and mercy shall follow me all the days of my life;
and I shall dwell in the house of the Lord for ever.
— Revised Standard Version of the Bible

Leader: What is your only comfort in life and in death?

All: **That I belong — body and soul, in life and death —**
not to myself but to my faithful Savior, Jesus Christ.
— Question 1, Heidelberg Catechism, adapt.

Leader: Let us pray.
O God whose ways are not our ways,
and whose thoughts are not our thoughts:
we acknowledge that we are of dust and to dust we shall return.
We stand before the great mystery of life and death,
deeply aware of the shortness and uncertainty of our days on earth.

If life-support is to be withdrawn:

We now are faced with hard decisions that may hasten death.
We ask you to guide whatever actions shall be taken
and to accept whatever we must do as the best that human wisdom
and medical science at this time can determine as most humane.
Yet we see only in the mirror of finite distortions,
and we place ourselves into the hands of your mercy and grace.

In all situations the prayer continues:

We intercede for your servant _____,
thanking you for *his/her* life and for all that *he/she is*
to those who love *him/her.*
We now entrust *him/her* to you as *he/she* comes to meet you.
Be merciful to *him/her,* forgive *his/her* sin,
and grant to *him/her* the promise of life eternal in your realm.
Be with those who mourn, grant them the assurance of your presence,
and the promise of your healing love;
through Jesus Christ our Lord.

All: **Amen.**

Other prayers and intercessions may be offered.

Minister: As Jesus taught his disciples, we pray:

The Lord's Prayer may be prayed in any version or language or in the following ecumenical
version:

All: **Our Father in heaven:**
Hallowed be your name,
Your kingdom come,
Your will be done, on earth as in heaven.

> **Give us today our daily bread.**
> **Forgive us our sins, as we forgive those who sin against us.**
> **Save us from the time of trial, and deliver us from evil.**
> **For the kingdom, the power, and the glory are yours,**
> **now and forever. Amen.**

Leader: Hear the comforting assurance of our Savior:
            "Come to me, all you that are weary and are carrying heavy burdens,
            and I will give you rest."   — Matthew 11:28

If the person is to be anointed, the leader prays:

Leader: Bless this oil, O Christ, that it may be to *him/her*
            a sign of your redeeming love on the cross
            and of *his/her* oneness with you in your death
            and resurrection to eternal life.

All: **Amen.**

Leader: Into your hands, O merciful Savior,
            we commend your servant, _____ .

The leader may make the sign of the cross on the person's forehead, with or without the oil of anointing.

> Acknowledge, we humbly pray,
> a sheep of your own fold,
> a lamb of your own flock,
> and a *son/daughter* of your own redeeming.
> Receive *him/her* into the arms of your mercy,
> into the blessed rest of everlasting peace,
> and into the glorious company of the saints in light.

All: **Amen.**   — *Book of Common Prayer,* alt.

Leader: May the Lord bless you and take care of you;
            May the Lord be kind and gracious to you;
            May the Lord look on you with favor and give you peace.

All: **Amen.**   — Numbers 6:24–26, TEV

Chapter Eleven

Christian Burial

Including:

A Liturgy for Christian Burial

A Liturgy for the Committal

The turbulent 1960s brought many critiques of the American way of life as well as the American way of death. Through the publication of a number of books that castigated us about our perceptions and practices surrounding death, we were jostled into an awareness that something was amiss. Funeral directors became defensive and asserted they only fulfilled the desires of the family. Clergy, determined to change things overnight, sometimes demanded practices that, although noble in intent, intruded on families' integrity at a time when they needed comfort, not ministerial rubrics regarding the funeral.

In the 1970s there emerged an awareness of the psychological and social dimensions of death and dying due to the publication of a number of studies and the introduction of university and high school courses on thanatology. Things having to do with death had a remarkable attraction to both young and old, and many local churches in some way or another offered courses on death and dying. The atmosphere was far more benign than it had been ten years earlier.

As society in the United States has become more increasingly secularized in the past twenty-five years and a larger percentage of the population faces death without faith traditions and faith communities, the practices surrounding the last rites for the dead more and more are being handled by the funeral industry. Whereas faith communities and their sacred spaces, burial rites, and pastoral leaders once were the norm, now complete funeral/memorial "packages," including the services of a religious officiant, are being marketed and sold ahead of need. Yet the practices and the words and actions we use to bury our dead have changed hardly a fraction. Often the funeral director has become the scapegoat for the lack of change. However, we must remember that the funeral industry is providing a service and can market only what people want. And what people want in the funeral business is generally what they have been accustomed to.

Clergy, including me, have sought to be change agents, yet we too need to be reminded that change cannot take place simply by our insisting on certain practices when we meet with the family to make plans for a funeral service — if we can get to the family *before* the funeral director! Since families rarely plan for funerals ahead of time, the survivors are forced to piece together a patchwork based on things intimated by the deceased over the years. Once death has initiated the grief process, the family generally turns to what is familiar and secure in their cultural awareness. Most often a minister's suggestions to depart from the norms that local *Mishnas* have legitimized are just too threatening. If change — and I prefer to call it renewal — is to take place, it will be meaningful and lasting only if it is initiated long before a family needs, within a few hours, to make all the arrangements for the funeral of their loved one. Thus, the church by precept and example has the mandate to help people recognize that, in addition to writing a will to put our earthly house in order, we also must determine before death the practices and liturgies that will be part of our departures from this world. The funeral industry, for other reasons, has realized the value of preplanning and has taken to TV commercials to convince us of it.

Hence I feel it unwise to chisel off the tremendous weight of cultural overlay with the sharp blows of ecclesiastical hammers. Rather, I would like to peer underneath the overlay with a fluoroscopic kind of vision and try to discover what motivates our liturgies for the burial of the dead. If in the process we find a truly significant theological modality, that modality will seep through the overlay with a freshness that, through time and interpretation, will bring renewal to our funeral practices and new meaning to the words and actions we use when one of our number passes from life to death to resurrection.

Although funeral practices vary from place to place, I have the notion that conceptually many Protestant funeral/memorial services are simply extensions of the viewing or concluding rites to a wake. The mourners gather around the open casket and are greeted by well-wishers. The body of the deceased is displayed, prompting the visitors to remark, "Doesn't he look nice!" When the service gets going, all quietly sit in their seats while the minister alone holds forth for the locally prescribed time deemed appropriate for such rites, prefacing a eulogy with some readings from canonical Scripture, sometimes reciting noncanonical poems which he or she has collected over the years, and concluding with a lengthy prayer that causes the mourners to shift in their seats. After the service, the visitors are asked by the mortician to say good-bye, not to the family but to the corpse. Sometimes in the presence of the onlookers the family must preside over the closing of the casket, and all then go to their cars. While most speed off back to work, the remnant of the family goes to the cemetery to inter the body, having to face the grief alone, surrounded only by the floral remembrances. What is all of this but a *viewing* with funeral exercises appended? How can the comforting assurance of the Gospel's words of resurrection take root in the grieving if they are disrupted by the wrenching experience of closing the casket after the service? An obituary advertising that "viewing will take place from 1:00 p.m. until the time of the service" always serves to confirm the suspicion in me that many funerals are simply viewings extended and appended with clerical rites that announce when the viewing is over.

I don't want to appear as harsh as my words may well seem. I don't want to put funeral directors out of business, for they do perform a very needed and valuable service. I don't intend to eliminate the viewing of the body, for the family needs to see the body, especially in an age when people rarely die at home with the family surrounding them and when immediate cremation is becoming more the norm in a secularized society. The family also needs some setting in which friends can console them and in which they can tell the story often enough so that death can become a reality to them. I don't want to put florists out of business either, for I, too, like flowers. But I do believe we need to search for a modality for the burial of the dead that grows out of the Christian faith itself and fulfills the needs of those facing the trauma of death.

Paul, writing to the Romans, said, "For I am convinced that neither death, nor life . . . nor things present, nor things to come . . . will be able to separate us from the love of God in Christ Jesus our Lord" (Romans 8:38–39). These words, which have become standard fare for many a funeral service, contain the two words central to Paul's theology: *in Christ,* an all-encompassing term for the totality of Christian existence. One's being *in Christ* is a total infusion into the very person of the risen Christ, who becomes the source, the reason, the meaning, and the goal of existence: "It is no longer I who live, but it is Christ who lives in me" (Galatians 2:20). Moreover, being *in Christ* is a state of being not restricted by the boundaries of birth and death but established "before the foundation of the world . . . as a plan for the fullness of time" (Ephesians 1:4ff.). Hence, for those who are *in Christ* there is no separation of life and death. It is in this affirmation that we find, I believe, the theological modality upon which our burial practices and the liturgies for this act need to be built.

There are some who may question again the validity of designating burial as an act equivalent to baptism and the Eucharist. However, if what happens in death is the establishing of a new relationship in Christ by the grace of God, and if the liturgical expression of this action is more than a mere extension of a viewing of the corpse, then I am willing to adopt such a designation. God acts in death to bring about a new relationship; the resurrection body is a new gift of God. If a sacramental act is one that cannot be without the actions of God, it seems to me that the celebration of God's resurrecting power certainly is worthy of such a designation. However, to those more comfortable with the traditional restriction to only two sacraments, perhaps regarding the act of burial as an extension of baptism, in which one has already been buried and raised in Christ, will be more satisfying.

Some also may deem the designation "burial" too restrictive in an age when other means of disposition of the body are increasingly popular. The word "burial" here is *theological* language for a reality initiated by God, like that of baptism, in which we are buried *in Christ* and raised *in Christ* to new life. In that sense, burial in Christ at baptism is the sign of the ultimate burial of our body and the gift of a new resurrected body. Burial with Christ in baptism is an initiation into the new life of Christ, and the burial with Christ at death is the fulfillment of life in Christ. Both are acts of grace, and both could not be without the action of a gracious God. If it may be less confusing to a public curious about what happened or shall happen to the corpse, the service, in instances where the body is not present or is to be cremated later, may be designated as a memorial service or a funeral service. Regardless of the label and the means of disposition, the divine action we celebrate is the same.

To symbolize the reality that in baptism we are, *in Christ,* in a new relationship with each other that continues even in death, the minister may stand at the font for the beginning and conclusion of the funeral/memorial service. One who has been baptized in Christ does not terminate membership in the church at death as our funeral liturgies so woefully seem to connote. Why are we so certain of the validity of praying for a person before he or she dies and then so afraid both to pray for God's blessing upon him or her after death or to pray for a continued relationship with the person even in death? Maybe it's not so much a matter of our theological reservations about notions of purgatory — the traditional excuse — as it is simply a matter that we are afraid of death! If we could assure ourselves that the act of burial is a sure sign of God's action that, rather than terminating our relationship with each other, unites us even more in the larger communion of all who have lived and died in Christ, perhaps we wouldn't let our hearts be so troubled and afraid. Of course, that's a matter of faith, not of liturgics. Nevertheless, liturgies do strengthen our faith.

If what has just been said makes any sense at all, then it appears to me we have a wholly different modality for the act of Christian burial. It won't be a morbid appendix to the viewing of the body, but the joyous Easter affirmation that one who has lived and died in Christ is indeed raised from the dead. Some may think it presumptuous to make such an affirmation about someone whose frailties we have known. But the early church knew the human shortcomings of it members, yet was bold enough to affirm that by baptism and by the promise of God their deceased member would indeed be granted the crown of everlasting righteousness. Paul, for example, knew well what was going on in Corinth, yet he could make some very bold affirmations to the Corinthian church about the meaning and the certainty of the resurrection. Like Paul, I hope we can begin to lose some of our timidity and can affirm in the act of burial the joyous certainties we say we believe.

To say that we affirm the certainty of resurrection is not to take death less seriously. On the contrary, we believe that Easter's certainty can dawn only through the reality of Good Friday's finality. The early creedal formulas insisted on preserving the reality of Jesus' death — he "suffered . . . was crucified . . . died . . . was buried." So, too, the act of burial needs to express the reality and finality of death: of the deceased person's and our own. Words such as "asleep" or "passed away" and other euphemistic avoidances help neither the bereaved nor us deal constructively with death. If we are truly in Christ, then we can *die* in Christ, just as we live in Christ and are resurrected in Christ. Closing the casket before the service, and not just at the beginning of the service, helps to bring about a realization of death's finality.

This is not to say that the finality of death does not elicit human feelings of grief, for indeed death does, and these emotions must be taken seriously. To act as though grief is unreal or, worse yet, to intimate that grief is the result of the lack of faith is being horribly callous. Death is a separation in familiarities, and this loss is real. Grief cannot be covered over. The family grieves, the church grieves, and both family and church need the reassurance that grief is very human and that consolation and healing will come by the promise and power of God. Just as our prayers and other liturgical expressions must reflect the reality of the resurrection, so also must they respond to the reality of human grief. And if the church is truly a caring community, the burden of that grief needs to be shared by the whole community. It seems to me that a meal would be a very natural extension of the liturgical act. At the meal, which the church can provide in the church facilities or in the family's home, family ties can be renewed and the church can be a supportive community. There is a sacramental dimension to such a meal that brings healing and renews *koinonia*.

The act of Christian burial also has a very personal dimension about it. I was once asked as I was making arrangements with a family for a funeral, "Will you mention Daddy's name?" Unfortunately, there have been many funerals in which the name of the person who died has never been mentioned. Perhaps in our attempts to be egalitarian and in reaction against some of the maudlin eulogies of the past, we have stuck by the book, thereby ignoring the uniqueness of the person who has died and the personal identification so needed by the family. The name of the person and his or her contribution to the life of the family, the church, and the community need to be remembered, for it is in remembering that we are at one with that person, and it is in remembering that the healing of grief begins. We are named and identified in baptism, and our name needs to be remembered in death also.

On the other hand, this order does not presuppose a eulogy or lengthy "remembrances" by family members and mourners who are invited "to come to the microphone" to share, sometimes laden with tears, their individual remembrances of sometimes trivial incidents in their personal relationships with the one who has died. Such eulogizing either by the minister or by a collection of individual speakers only fosters the notion that this is really a wake, especially if such remembrances are shared *after* Scripture and sermon. Eulogies are what secular societies give to fallen heroes under the assumption that the lingering effects of good and noble deeds guarantee immortality. Unfortunately I have been to many funeral/memorial services in which far more of the service is dedicated to remembering the one who died and extolling his or her virtues than to witnessing to the Gospel's resurrection promise. Instead, I suggest that the appropriate and necessary remembering occur within the context of a sermon or homily that, based on the Scriptures, proclaims the good news of resurrection in Christ. One's being in Christ will reflect itself in one's words and deeds, and their remembrance is a concrete illustration, from the life of the person, of what it means to be *in Christ*. If a brief time of eulogizing is needed, then such may be offered by a person so designated by the family to do so — at the beginning of the service *before* Scripture and sermon, as indicated in the accompanying liturgy. It is important that remembrances be scripted, brief, and very limited, perhaps to just one offered by a representative person. To avoid the appearance that a funeral service is "canned," it seems more appropriate to read the Scripture directly from the Bible, rather than from a manual or service book. These lessons may be chosen by the minister in consultation with the family. Members of the family or of the church may read the lessons.

The rubrics of the model that follows suggest that a member of the congregation participate in the words of the committal to symbolize that the whole church, who received this person in baptism, now commends him or her to God in Christ. Sadly, most funeral services I have been a part of have been, to the last word, totally clerically oriented. We need to rediscover that the *whole church* participates in the life and death experience; that realization can bring about an entirely new dimension of the church's support to those facing death and to their families as well.

We live in an era in which funerals often have their settings in neither the home of the deceased nor in a church but in a funeral parlor. This setting tends to foster the idea that the funeral is an extension of the viewing. But to mandate, by pastoral decree, that all funerals be held in the church is rather ill-advised, and the families generally are not ready for such an immediate change in their perceptions. I often have heard families express that they do not want the service in the church for fear that every time they worship, they will have mental flashbacks of the funeral. Although that is the wrong reason for not having the service in the church and the idea of remembering a loved one in the context of worship is quite appropriate, and even though the casket need not be present in the sanctuary nor even in the church building, we are going to have to live with the reality that for some time in some communities the funeral parlor will continue to be perceived as the most appropriate setting for funerals. Although families who have been part of memorial services in which the casket was not present are sometimes more ready to accept the idea of having the service in the church, only through a gradual process of education by precept and example will we once again see the church as the fitting setting for the funeral of one who was initiated into the church through baptism and is entrusted to God by the church in death. Incidentally, one reason why funerals sometimes are not held in churches is that the architecture of many church buildings militates against doing so. Steps, narrow aisles, fixed pews, lack of facilities for the family to gather in a friendly setting to receive visitors prior to the service, and many other factors continue to foster the idea that a funeral home is a more hospitable setting for a funeral service.

Therefore, our liturgies for the act of burial will need to be flexible enough to accommodate to the setting and, by their educative nature, will have to serve as transitional orders. Even though many funerals will continue to be set in funeral parlors in the foreseeable future, there is no reason why liturgical renewal cannot take place in that setting as well as in the church. Bulletins with the order of worship and some information regarding the person who has died can be used for a service even in a funeral home. At least in the areas in which I have served pastorates, people desire some kind of remembrance of the funeral, and since the church generally hasn't provided one, funeral directors have filled the void with little cards listing vital statistics regarding the deceased. It seems far more appropriate, however, to retain as a remembrance the words and acts that were said and done together at the time of a person's death and burial. Since the orders for burial are not included in many Protestant hymnals, there is no way for anyone to know either ahead of time or following the funeral what really is part of the act. Thus bulletins for funeral services can fulfill a number of needs very simply. And inasmuch as bulletins also have educational value, I believe that, as people periodically sift through the things they have accumulated and come across the bulletins they have stashed away in dresser drawers, we will see a gradual liturgical renewal take place. Whether the burial service is held in the church or in the funeral home, bulletins enable the congregation to be participants in, rather than mere spectators of, the liturgical action. Such participation can bring about a realization that the act of burial is something quite different from a mere extension of the viewing. The liturgical expressions in this chapter are included in the accompanying CD-ROM to facilitate insertion into bulletins.

One mode of participation that ought to be restored to its rightful place in funeral services is singing — not the morose doggerel that, in the popular mind, is associated with old-time funerals, but the singing of the great hymns of the faith that affirm God's action and are sources of comfort. In some studies of lay theology, people have responded to theological questions with direct quotes from hymns. If theological understandings are to assist people in their grief, why not include some of the sources of those understandings in the service? Even if some families have reservations about singing, and even when not enough people are present to facilitate singing, the use of responsive or unison readings of the Psalms can serve the same function as song. The model order that follows is filled intentionally with language lifted directly from the Psalms, hymns, and other quite familiar liturgical acts.

There are times when the minister is called upon to officiate at burial services for people who have not been part of the life of the congregation. I am not speaking about what a friend of mine calls "rent-a-preacher" services, but the times at which families of nonmembers earnestly desire the ministrations of the church upon the death of one of their number. Often there is a lot of guilt mingled with the grief in these situations, and the minister and the church need to be sensitive to these families' needs and emotions, and must be willing to be supportive regardless of membership status. The promise of at-one-ness in paradise given by Jesus on the cross was a gift not to the faithful, but to the one who was condemned and hanged along with him. Therefore, we cannot be judgmental in our relationships upon the death of nonmembers, nor can we be artificial in our liturgical expressions. In the liturgy in this chapter, I have attempted to provide a number of alternative expressions, and the minister needs to use discretion in selecting what is appropriate in the particular situation.

With the increased awareness of the alternative modes of disposition of the body, we need to ensure that our liturgical expressions are flexible enough to accommodate any departures from the usual practices. The following order attempts to provide alternative expressions for a variety of situations. Despite my aversion to them, the many rubrics included in the order are necessary to indicate the different directions the services may take.

It is certainly appropriate for the Eucharist to be celebrated as part of the act of Christian burial if the service is held in the church. It was the Last Supper that prepared Jesus' disciples for his death, and it was in the breaking of the bread that the risen Christ was made known to them on the day of resurrection. Since we are bound together in Christ in communion in the saints, what better way to realize this union than in the act of *communing*? Protestants need to rediscover what other sectors of the church have known for centuries about the healing power of Christ in the Eucharist to nourish and sustain God's people in the midst of death. The following liturgy includes the celebration of the Eucharist. If Eucharist is not celebrated, the service concludes as indicated in the rubrics. All expressions are included in the accompanying CD-ROM.

Finally, some brief directions are in order regarding the following liturgy. Generally, the order is designed to be used in all settings. However, those expressions that involve congregational participation are designed for a setting in which a bulletin is printed. Others do not involve spoken or sung participation by a congregation. The leader will need to decide which of the alternatives are to be used. Each is separated by an *"or"* in the liturgy. This order may be used in its entirety, or various elements can be incorporated into familiar services. The order also includes the opportunity for creedal affirmations, if such are deemed appropriate. A setting of Psalm 23, sung or spoken, either as a unison or responsive affirmation may be substituted for a creed. A setting of the *Te Deum* or a Psalm or canticle are other good alternatives.

The order presumes that whether the service is held in the church or in the funeral home, the casket will be closed at a time prior to, and preferably not immediately before, the service, and not in the presence of the congregation. In the church it is appropriate for the casket to be covered with a pall, which is a more powerful symbol than a floral spray. A pall can be made or purchased by the church and used for the act of burial of all members, thereby expressing that all are united in Christ through a common baptism, regardless of their status in life or the wherewithal of their estate to provide a casket commensurate with that status. The minister and members of the family may place the pall on the casket after the *asperges* (sprinkling.)

We have a long road to travel before such expressions and practices are incorporated into the life of the church. That pilgrimage cannot be hurried or forced. The order that follows is but one attempt to chart that course.

A LITURGY FOR CHRISTIAN BURIAL
CD-ROM 11.1.1

Minister: Let us worship God and remember _____ .

And

Minister: The Lord is risen!

All: **He is risen indeed!**

Minister: Whoever is in Christ is a new creation.

All: **The old has passed away: behold, the new has come.**

Or

Minister: Our help is in the name of the Lord.

All: **Who made heaven and earth.**

A hymn celebrating the resurrection may be sung. If the casket is to be carried into the church, the pallbearers may bring it to the font during the singing of the hymn.

A paschal candle may be lighted and placed near the font and casket.

The minister may stand at the font, dip a branch into the water, and sprinkle water on the casket or urn, saying:

Minister: All of us who have been baptized into Christ Jesus
          were baptized into his death.
          Therefore we have been buried with him by baptism into death,
          so that, just as Christ was raised from the dead by the glory of the Father,
          so we too might walk in newness of life.   — Romans 6:3–4, adapt.

A pall may be placed on the casket.

Minister: Let us pray.

All: **O God, our Alpha and Omega, we bless you for our beginning
          and give thanks for our baptism into your everlasting covenant.
          We remember all the blessings that accompany each day of our lives.
          We are comforted that in life and in death we belong not to ourselves
          but to our faithful savior Jesus Christ.
          Open our sorrowed hearts and our troubled minds
          to receive the wondrous promises of your grace,
          that we who die with Christ on the cross
          may live with him in your kingdom that has no end. Amen.**

Or

Minister: Let us pray.
          O God who is Alpha and Omega, our beginning and our end,
          we give you humble thanks that by our baptism
          into the death of your Son, Jesus Christ,
          we who are buried with him
          may also be raised with him to newness of life.
          By your Holy Spirit, open our hearts and minds
          to receive in faith the assurance of the communion of saints,
          the forgiveness of sins, and the resurrection to life eternal.

All: **Amen.**

Or

Minister: Let us pray.
O God, our refuge and our strength,
we turn to you our helper in the time of our trouble.
By the comforting words of the Scriptures,
and by your presence here among us,
enable us to receive the assurance
that even though death crosses our lives,
the victory of Jesus Christ over death and the grave
may give us also the promise of resurrection
to everlasting life in his name.

All: **Amen.**

Or

Minister: Let us pray.
Creator of a season and a time for everything under heaven —
a time to be born, and a time to die —
help us to accept the reality of this time of death,
but open us also by your Holy Spirit to behold your promise
of that other reality which lies beyond death's time,
through the resurrection of your Son, Jesus Christ.

All: **Amen.**

If brief remembrances are to be shared by members of the family or the faith community, they may be included here, prefaced by the following invitation. If no remembrances are to be included, the service continues with the reading of the Scripture lessons.

Minister: In the act of remembering, we are at one with all the saints
who surround us as a great cloud of witnesses.
Remembrances of (*Name*) _____ will be shared by
(*Name*) _____ .

The minister or a reader continues with the following prayer for illumination:

Minister/Reader:
Let us pray.
From the beginning your Word, O God,
has been the life and the light of all people,
shining in darkness but never overcome by darkness.
Illumine again our reading and hearing of your Word,
that we may receive light for our journey
through these valleys of shadows,
and the promise of new life through our Lord Jesus Christ. Amen.

Scripture texts from the Old and New Testaments are read. Suggested lections are:

Old Testament

        Isaiah 25:6–9

        Isaiah 40:1–2a, 6, 8 (Upon the death of a child, verse 11 may be added.)

        Lamentations 3:22–26, 31–33

Between the lessons the following Psalms may be sung or said responsively: Psalm 23; Psalm 46; Psalm 90:1–4, 12–17, Psalm 121; Psalm 139:1–18, 23–24. Following the Psalm, a setting of the Gloria Patri may be sung or spoken.

Epistles

        Romans 8:31–35, 37–39

        1 Corinthians 15:1–5 or 1 Corinthians 15:20–24

        Revelation 22:1–4 or Revelation 22:1–5

After the lesson(s), the following may be said:

Reader: The grass withers, the flower fades,

All: **but the word of our God will stand forever.**   —Isaiah 40:8

Gospels

        Mark 10:13–16 (upon the death of a child)

        John 11:17–27

        John 14:1–6a, 15–17, 25–27

The reading of the Gospel lesson may be prefaced and appended by the following. The congregation may stand for the reading of the Gospel.

Reader: The good news of Christ is recorded in the Gospel according
           to _____, the _____ chapter, beginning to read at the _____
           verse.

All: **Glory be to you, O Lord.**

The Gospel lesson is read.

Reader: This is the Gospel.

All: **Praise be to you, O Christ.**

A homily or sermon is preached.

A creed or statement of faith may be affirmed in unison, prefaced by the following:

Minister: Let us join with all the saints who have lived and died in Christ and boldly
           affirm:

All: **I believe in God . . .**

If a creed is omitted, and if Psalm 23 has not been read as one of the Old Testament lessons, the minister or congregation may say either responsively or in unison:

All: The Lord is my shepherd, I shall not want;
           He makes me lie down in green pastures.
           He leads me beside still waters; he restores my soul.
           He leads me in paths of righteousness for his name's sake.
           Even though I walk through the valley of the shadow of death,
               I fear no evil.
           For you are with me: Your rod and your staff, they comfort me.
           You prepare a table before me in the presence of my enemies;
           You anoint my head with oil, my cup overflows.
           Surely, goodness and mercy shall follow me all the days of my life;
           And I shall dwell in the house of the Lord forever.

                                        —Psalm 23, adapted from RSV

A hymn or a setting of the Gloria Patri may be sung or spoken.

Minister: In peace, and for the peace which passes all understanding,
            let us pray to the God of peace.

Minister: O God, who in Christ Jesus has called us from death to life:
            We praise you for the promises of baptism
            assuring us that we are your sons and daughters,
            children of your everlasting covenant
            through the death and resurrection of our Lord Jesus Christ.
            We thank you for giving us [*baptized name(s)*] ——————————
            as our *brother/sister* in the household of faith,
            and we remember with joy *his/her* days among us.

Other attributes may be remembered.

            And we pray that as you gave *him/her* life,
            now in death you will receive *him/her*
            into the blessed peace that passes our understanding.

All: Grant to us and to all people the assurance
           that neither death nor life,
           nor things present, nor things to come
           will be able to separate us from your love
           which is in Christ Jesus our Lord.
           Enable us so to live in Christ,
           that when we have fought the good fight,
           finished our race, and kept the faith,
           you will grant to us also
           the crown of righteousness and heavenly reunion.

Or

Minister: God of grace and mercy, we praise you
that through the death and resurrection of your Son,
Jesus Christ, we are born to a new and living hope.

On the death of a child:

As he took little children into his arms, receive now
this child into the arms of your parenting mercy, and assure
(*Names of parents and other immediate family members*)
_____ that your blessing rests upon *him/her*
in the family of heaven.

On the death of an adult:

We thank you especially for (*name*) _____,
for the gift of *his/her* life, and for your grace given *him/her.*
We pray that you will receive *him/her* into the arms of your mercy
and into the blessed peace that passes our understanding.

By the power of your Holy Spirit,
continue to reassure us that neither death nor life,
nor things present, nor things to come
will be able to separate us from your love
which is in Christ Jesus our Lord.
Enable us so to live in Christ,
that when we have fought the good fight,
finished our race, and kept the faith, you will grant to us also
the crown of righteousness and heavenly reunion.

The minister may pray any or all of the following petitions and/or intercessions.

Minister: O God, though our vision is clouded by the burden of grief
and our understanding distorted by the uncertainties of the future,
break through the darkness that seems to overwhelm us
with a love that will not let us go.

Good Shepherd, lead (*name[s] of the grieving*) _____ / *us*
through the valleys of shadows, comfort *them/us*
in the midst of the things *they/we* cannot understand,
support *them/us* in *their/our* needs,
and assure *them/us* of your enduring patience
and your healing presence.

Give to us in the household of faith the compassion
to share *his/her/their* grief, to understand *his/her/their* needs,
and to sustain *him/her/them* in this hour of trial
and throughout our pilgrimage together as the church of Jesus Christ.

All: **Amen.**

If the Eucharist is to be celebrated, the service continues with the following. If not, or if this is a graveside service only, the liturgy continues with the Lord's Prayer and concluding rites below.

Eucharist
CD-ROM 11.1.2

Minister: Lift up your hearts!

All: **We lift them to the God of our salvation.**

Minister: O God who broke through the shadows of death
           with resurrection joy,
           we lift our hearts in the assurance
           that because Jesus lives we shall live also,
           and that neither life nor death
           nor things present nor things to come
           can separate us from your love for us.

           We remember that on the night before his death,
           Jesus took bread, and blessed, and broke it,
           and gave it to the disciples and said,
           "Take, eat, this is my body."
           And he took a cup, and when he had given thanks,
           he gave it to them, saying,
           "Drink of it, all of you, for this is my blood of the new covenant
           which is poured out for many for the forgiveness of sins.
           I tell you I shall not drink again of this fruit of the vine
           until that day when I drink it new with you
           in my father's kingdom."

           We remember also that on the day of resurrection,
           when Christ was at table with two of the disciples,
           he took the bread, blessed and broke it and gave it to them;
           and their eyes were opened, and they recognized him.

           In remembering, unite us sacramentally in Christ's resurrected life.
           Bless us and this bread and wine we offer you,
           that we may be nourished through these holy mysteries until
           we feast at last in the full communion of all the saints. Amen.

All: *speaking*
           Christ has died!
           Christ has risen!
           Christ will come again!

Or singing (the accompaniment is on page 170).

Christ has died, Christ is ris - en, Christ will come a - gain!

Music: F. Russell Mitman, 2005

Minister: *breaking the bread*
            The bread which we break is a means of sharing in the body of Christ.

            pouring the cup
            The cup of blessing we bless is a means of sharing in the blood of Christ.

All pray the Lord's Prayer.

Minister: This is the feast of remembrance of Christ's death and resurrection
            in which he promises his sacred presence.
            All who desire are invited to receive the bread and cup,
            and may come to the *chancel/stations* to receive them.
            It is also a time for all of us to remember (*Name*) _____
            and to give quiet thanksgivings to God
            for the ways in which *he/she* touched our lives
            and in remembrance is at one with us.

Minister: *administering the bread*
            Jesus said, "Blessed are those who mourn, for they shall be comforted."
            This is the bread of heaven given for you.

            administering the cup
            Jesus said, "You have sorrow now, but I will see you again
            and your hearts will rejoice, and no one will take your joy from you."
            This is the cup of salvation given for you.

After all have communed the service continues with the following thanksgiving:

Minister: Behold, the dwelling of God is with mortals;
            God will dwell with them as their God;
            they will be God's people, and God will be with them;
            God will wipe every tear from their eyes.
            Death will be no more;
            mourning and crying and pain will be no more,
            for the former things have passed away.   — Revelation 21:3b–4

And/Or

Minister: Salvation belongs to our God who is seated on the throne
            and to the Lamb!

All: **Blessing and glory and wisdom and thanksgiving**
            and honor and power and might be to our God
            forever and ever! Amen.   — Revelation 7:10, 12, adapt.

Without Eucharist

If Eucharist is not celebrated, the service continues with:

Minister: Keep us constant in prayer, and hear us as we pray
as our Lord taught us:

All: **Our Father in heaven,
hallowed be your Name,
your kingdom come,
your will be done, on earth as it is in heaven.
Give us today our daily bread.
Forgive us our sins as we forgive those who sin against us.
Save us from the time of trial, and deliver us from evil.
For the kingdom, the power, and the glory are yours,
now and forever. Amen.**

Both Settings

Minister: *standing at the font or at the head of the casket*
Lord, now let your servant depart in peace, according to your word.

All: **For our eyes have seen your salvation.**   —Luke 2:29–30, adapt.

Minister: To the mercy of God and in the hope of resurrection to eternal life,
we commend (*Name*) _____ , our *brother/sister* in Christ.
Rest eternal grant to *him/her,* O God,
and let perpetual light shine upon *him/her.*

All: **Amen.**

A doxology, may be sung or said.

Minister: The peace which passes all understanding
keep your hearts and minds in Christ Jesus our Lord.

All: **Amen.**

And/Or

Minister: *while making the sign of the cross*
The blessing of God Almighty,
Father, Son, and Holy Spirit,
rest and abide with you now and forever.

All: **Amen.**

A hymn such as "For All the Saints" may be sung, and the casket or urn may be carried out of the church.

If this order is used for a graveside service alone, the service continues:

Minister: Holy One, whose Son on the cross placed his spirit into your hands,
we now commend (*Name*) _____ ,
our brother/our sister in Christ
Or (Name), this child in Christ,
into your everlasting care,
in the hope of resurrection through our Lord Jesus Christ.
And as Joseph laid the mortal body of our Lord into the sepulcher,
so, too, we commit the *body/ashes* of *our brother/our sister/this child*
to the ground/its final resting place.
O death, where is your sting?
O grave, where is your victory?
Thanks be to God who gives us the victory
through our Lord Jesus Christ. — 1 Corinthians 15:55–57, adapt.

May the God of peace
who brought back from the dead our Lord Jesus,
the great shepherd of the sheep,
by the blood of the eternal covenant
make you complete in everything good
so that you may do God's will, working among you
that which is pleasing in God's sight,
through Jesus Christ, to whom be the glory for ever and ever. Amen.
 — Hebrews 13:20–21, adapt.

Let us go in peace.

A LITURGY FOR THE COMMITTAL
CD-ROM 11.1.3

This order maybe used for an act of burial prior to a memorial service or for interment of the body or ashes following the service.

Minister: Grace to you and peace from God the Father,
and from our Lord Jesus Christ. — Romans 1:7b

Or

Peace to all of you who are in Christ. — 1 Peter 5:14

Minister or Reader:
Hear the comforting words of our Lord Jesus Christ:
"Very truly, I tell to you,
unless a grain of wheat falls into the earth and dies,
it remains just a single grain;

but if it dies, it bears much fruit.
Whoever serves me must follow me;
and where I am, there will my servant be also."   —John 12:24, 26

And/Or

"I am the resurrection and the life.
Those who believe in me, even though they die, will live;
and every one who lives and believes in me will never die."
       —John 11:25–26

Minister: Let us pray.

Minister: Holy One, whose Son on the cross placed his spirit into your hands,
we now commend (*Name*) _____,
our brother/our sister/this child in Christ into your everlasting care,
in the hope of resurrection through our Lord Jesus Christ.

Minister or Member of the Congregation:
And as Joseph laid the mortal body of our Lord into the sepulcher,
so, too, we commit the *body/ashes* of *our brother/our sister/this child*
to *the ground/its final resting place.*
Earth to earth, ashes to ashes, dust to dust.

Earth may be placed on the casket/urn.

Minister: Rest eternal grant to *him/her,* O Lord,
And let perpetual light shine upon *him/her*! Amen.

And/Or

Minister: Bless *him/her* and take care of *him/her,*
Be kind and gracious to *him/her,*
Look on *him/her* with favor, and give *him/her* peace. Amen.
      —Numbers 6:24–26, adapt., TEV

O death, where is your sting?
O grave, where is your victory?
Thanks be to God who gives us the victory
through our Lord Jesus Christ.   —1 Corinthians 15:55–57, adapt.

Minister: Let us give thanks.
We thank you, O God, that in Christ
you triumphed over death and the grave, assuring us and all people
of the resurrection to eternal life.

We ask you to give to (*Name*) _____
the heavenly crown of life and the fulfillment of all the blessings
you promised *him/her* on earth.

We pray for the comforting presence of your Holy Spirit
to be with and all who mourn, that in the midst of grief and pain,
they may be touched with heaven's peace and healing.

Make us deeply aware of the precariousness of human life,
and keep us in communion with all who have lived and died in Christ,
that we may live in faith and hope until in death you receive us home
and unite us with the whole family of heaven;
through the glory and to the honor of Jesus Christ. Amen.

Or

Receive, Eternal God, our joyous thanks,
that we who are baptized into the death and resurrection of your Son,
Jesus Christ, may share with him, both in life and in death,
the promise of eternal life.

Give to (*Name*) _____ in death
the continued blessings you showered upon *him/her* in life,
and grant to us the assurance that whether we live or die,
we belong to you in the blessed communion of all the saints;
through Jesus Christ our Lord. Amen.

Or

O God, by the death of your Son, Jesus,
you have taken away the sting of death, and by his rest in the tomb
you have blessed the graves of all your people.
Receive our joyous thanks for his victory over death
and for the promise that all who live and die in Christ
may share in the resurrection to eternal life.
Keep us in communion with all who have lived and died,
and by your Holy Spirit enable us to continue our pilgrimage
in faith, hope, and love,
and at last be joined with the whole company of heaven;
through Jesus Christ. Amen.

The minister may offer the following or any other suitable blessing.

Minister: May the God of peace who brought back from the dead our Lord Jesus,
the great shepherd of the sheep, by the blood of the eternal covenant,
make you complete in everything good so that you may do his will,
working in you that which is pleasing in God's sight,
through Jesus Christ, to whom be the glory forever and ever. Amen.

—Hebrews 13:20–21, adapt.

Or

> May the God who gives us peace make you holy in every way
> and keep your whole being — spirit, soul, and body —
> free from every fault until the coming of Jesus Christ. Amen.
> — 1 Thessalonians 5:23, TEV, adapt.

Minister: Let us go in peace.

Appendix

ACCOMPANIMENTS

Doxology from Revelation

F. Russell Mitman, 2000

Bless-ing and glo - ry and wis-dom and thanks and hon - or and pow - er and might be to God for ev - er and ev - er more, for ev - er and ev - er more. A - men.

Memorial Acclamation

F. Russell Mitman, 2005

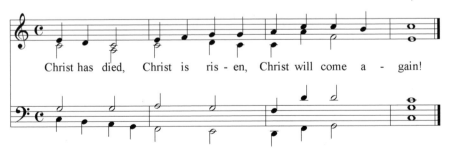

Christ has died, Christ is ris - en, Christ will come a - gain!

Psalm 139 Response

F. Russell Mitman, 2004

Lord, you have searched me and known me.

Kyrie

F. Russell Mitman, 2004

Lord, have mer - cy on us.

Christ, have mer - cy on us.

Lord, have mer - cy on us.

Psalm 16 Response

F. Russell Mitman, 2005

Pro - tect me, O God, for in you I take re - fuge.

Trisagion

F. Russell Mitman, 2005

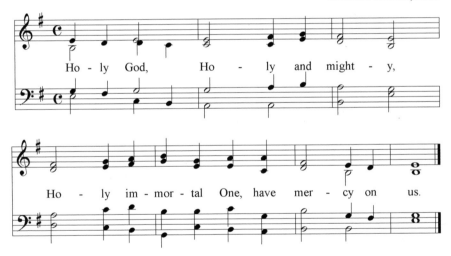

Ho - ly God, Ho - ly and might - y,

Ho - ly im - mor - tal One, have mer - cy on us.

Psalm 130

Words: Psalm 130:1–7; NRSV, alt.

F. Russell Mitman, 2005

Continued on next page

Psalm 130 (continued)

Continued on next page

Psalm 130 (continued)

The Choir may repeat the response
The Cantor alone may sing the response quietly.

Accompaniment for Stanzas
1 through 4 (minor key)

Words: Isaac Watts, 1709 alt.

MAUNDY 8.8.8.8
F. Russell Mitman, 2004

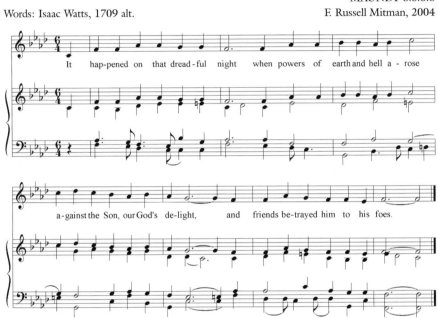

It hap-pened on that dread-ful night when powers of earth and hell a-rose

a-gainst the Son, our God's de-light, and friends be-trayed him to his foes.

Accompaniment for Stanza 5
(Major Key)

Isaac Watts, 1709 alt.

MAUNDY 8.8.8.8
F. Russell Mitman, 2004

O Lord, your feast we cel - e - brate; we show your death; we sing your name

till you re - turn, when we shall eat the mar - riage sup - per of the Lamb!

Prayer Response

F. Russell Mitman, 1987

In your mer - cy, O God, hear our prayer.

In your mer - cy, O God, hear our prayer, and grant us your peace. A - men.

Other Worship Resources from F. Russell Mitman, published by The Pilgrim Press

IMMERSED IN THE SPLENDOR OF GOD
Resources for Worship Renewal
Updated resources for the renewal of your church's worship life.
Contains a useful CD with fresh liturgies.
ISBN 0-8298-1614-3
Paper with CD, 208 pages, $25

WORSHIP IN THE SHAPE OF SCRIPTURE
Foreword by Marva J. Dawn
Guides readers through the practical steps of moving from lectionary to liturgy, focusing on text, structuring the worship service, writing vital liturgy, planning in advance for shared leadership, and actually leading worship.
ISBN 0-8298-1421-3
Paper, 176 pages, $16

Additional Worship Resources from The Pilgrim Press

BLESSING NEW VOICES
Prayers of Young People and Worship Resources for Youth Ministry
Maren C. Tirabassi
Best-selling author Tirabassi joins voices with more than 160 young writers ages 12–21 in an exciting medley of worship resources and prayers covering a wide range of topics.
ISBN 0-8298-1402-7
Paper, 144 pages, $10

GIFTS OF MANY CULTURES
Worship Resources for the Global Community
Maren C. Tirabassi and Kathy Wonson Eddy
A moving collection of liturgical resources from the global community that are designed to enrich worship, encourage cross-cultural appreciation, facilitate church mission programming, and deepen spiritual understanding across the global community.
ISBN 0-8298-1029-3
Paper, 272 pages, $20.00

Additional Worship Resources from The Pilgrim Press

HARVEST FOR THE WORLD
A Worship Anthology on Sharing in the Work of Creation
Compiled by Geoffrey Duncan
A colorful resource celebrating the goodness of creation and encouraging work toward an equitable distribution of the Earth's gifts.
ISBN 0-8298-1530-9
Paper, 304 pages, $21

HEALING WORSHIP
Purpose and Practice
Bruce G. Epperly
Shows how to incorporate various healing services into the total life of the congregation.
ISBN 978-0-8298-1742-3
Paper, 144 pages, $18

LET JUSTICE ROLL DOWN
A Worship Resource for Lent, Holy Week, and Easter
Compiled by Geoffrey Duncan
A collection of Lent, Holy Week, and Easter resources from around the world.
ISBN 0-8298-1633-X
Paper, 304 pages, $21

NURTURING FAITH AND HOPE
Black Worship as a Model for Christian Education
Anne E. Streaty Wimberly
Shares what can be learned about Christian education from the Black church worship experience.
ISBN 0-8298-1568-6
Paper, 208 pages, $18

PILGRIM PRAYERS FOR LEADING WORSHIP
John E. Biegert
Prayers to lead worship for all seasons and occasions.
ISBN 0-8298-1567-8
Paper, 128 pages, $10

SEVEN SONGS OF CREATION
Liturgies for Celebrating and Healing Earth
THE EARTH BIBLE
Norman C. Habel, ed.
Discover the living voice of Earth heard through liturgies and songs.
ISBN 0-8298-1593-7
Paper, 224 pages, $28

THANKS BE TO GOD
Prayers and Parables for Public Worship
Glen E. Rainsley
A collection of prayers and parables that will help readers and listeners recognize God in the midst of the ordinary.
ISBN 0-8298-1637-2
Paper, 160 pages, $21

WORSHIP IN THE SPIRIT OF JESUS
Theology, Liturgy, and Songs without Violence
Jack Nelson-Pallmeyer and Bret Hesla
Alternative theological understandings and worship resources rooted in the nonviolent spirit of Jesus.
ISBN 0-8298-1674-7
Paper with CD, 208 pages, $25

To order these or any other books from The Pilgrim Press,
call or write:

The Pilgrim Press
700 Prospect Avenue
Cleveland, OH 44115-1100

Phone orders: 800.537.3394 (M-F, 8:30am-4:30pm ET)
Fax orders: 216.736.2206

Please include shipping charges of $6.00 for the first book and 75 cents for each additional book.

Or order from our web site at www.thepilgrimpress.com

Prices subject to change without notice.